THE
SECRET WAR
INSIDE
FREEMASONRY

MIDDLE CHAMBER MEDIA PUBLICATIONS, 2014

Published by Middle Chamber Media
First Printing December, 2014
Copyright ©Frater X, 2014
All Rights Reserved

ISBN: 13:978-0692339787
10:0692339787

The Secret War Inside Freemasonry
By Frater X
Edited by Mater X
Front Cover Artwork by Daniel Lish
Back Cover Art and Jacket Design by Chris Vellrath

Printed in the United States of America

i

~For Ursa,

My darling Little Bear~

"...I have endeavored in the following sheets to represent some mistakes, irregularities, and unseemly transactions, which have been occasioned by the want of acquaintance with them; nor will the brethren, I hope, take it a miss, (as I have chosen TRUTH for my patron) that I should strictly adhere to its principles, and point out the base and impure from its generous and the brave's neither is it to be wondered at, that there are some of the former disposition amongst us, since experience evidently convinces that in all sects of men some impious and turbulent spirits appear, whose unlawful actions ought rather to be exposed than concealed, that they themselves may see their evil deeds in a proper light, and turn from their iniquities..."

~pg. 23; A Serious and Impartial Inquiry into the Cause of the Present Decay of Free-Masonry in the Kingdom of Ireland, 1744, by Fifield D'Assigny M.D.

CONTENTS

ACKNOWLEDGEMENTS

As with all artistic literary projects, especially among the working class of America, none of it could be accomplished or completed without the steadfast love, support, faith, and contribution of others. I would like to express my deepest appreciation to all who did just that with me, either mentioned here or not. Many thanks to Chuck Payne, Bob Sevigny and Joe Costa, three of my dearest companions and oldest friends; as well as Coulston and Gail Miller, Jack Reynolds, Chuck Laird, my mother Karen and my sister Chelsea, Mike and Sandy Ryland, the Kelley Family; also Freeman Fly and Jamie Hanshaw, Leo Rizzo, Swami Shivananda Giri, Mark Passio and Barb, Michael Falsetta, Chris Vellrath, Bob Tuskin, Fred Immendorfer, Psonik, Steve and Deb from Type1 Radio, Daniel Lish, Krista and Jimmy Ponte, Free Energy Jay; Jah's Dream and Train Wreck, Frank Herbert, Philip K. Dick, Douglas Adams, Robert Anton Wilson, Cystemic-Jeremy, Tim, and John, the MC5, Dead Kennedys, Social Distortion, Daft Punk, The Crystal Method, EDM and the Dubstep Revolution, Surf Rock; my Masonic mentors brothers and friends who remain nameless here: J∴D∴ W∴R∴ M∴G∴ B∴S∴, and to Brother Shane Merrifield and Brother James Wright. I would acknowledge as well Lon Milo Duquette and John Michael Greer, also John Lamb Lash, Israel Regardie, Arthur Waite, JSM Ward, Henry Coil Jr., Thomas Smith Webb, Jeremy Ladd Cross, and all the host of other Masonic authors I stumbled upon and feverishly devoured on my quest. To my benefactors Kirk Rhorer, Jamile Bassett and Jeff Woods, and most especially my uncle William M. Parker, thank you all for all you did to help me realize my lifelong dream. And finally, to my wife and co-conspirator, proof-reader and editor extraordinaire: Mater X, I could not have done the work I have these past 15 years without her standing beside me; and to our four children for all their love, support and sacrifice of me, and my time.

INTRODUCTION

I have been preparing for this book my entire adult life. I began my obsession with Freemasonry during my time studying at University of Massachusetts Harbor Campus in Boston. Having run the gambit of Eastern studies in Philosophy and Mysticism, I found myself on the backdoor step of Western Tradition, so to speak, searching for the "Great Western Esoteric Mystical Zeitgeist", the lost spirit of Western Mysticism; my own Grail Quest. My Eastern studies in Hinduism, Taoism, and most especially Zen Buddhism, had me painfully aware that besides the strong over-bearing church traditions and oppositional stances to them, there was a vacuum in Western Spirituality; an absence of sacred tradition and a gap in continuity, within my own psyche as well as within the very Western Culture of my upbringing.

During my time at University, my step-father joined the local "Blue Lodge", or Lodge of Ancient Free and Accepted Masons (AF&AM), in our colonial New England hometown. A series of synchronous events converged at this time in my awareness, events which I view now as signals of something significant, lurking imperceptible, just outside the field of everyday consciousness. President George H.W. Bush, former Director of the CIA, had prosecuted the speediest war in history with Operation Desert Storm the first Gulf War in Iraq. He announced the ushering in of the New World Order on Sept. 11th 1991, and then onto a new President. The Unabomber printed his manifesto in the NY Times, OJ Simpson was acquitted, Waco burned to the ground, and Oklahoma City blew up.

It was the 90's and President Clinton led the hedonism- parade like some post-modern pied-piper; I can still see Hilary and the Gores dancing on Inauguration Night, with Bill playing his Sax and Fleetwood Mac singing in the background *"...don't stop thinking about tomorrow..."*. The myth of progress was wearing thin but we all jumped in the pool anyway, and let the warm chemically treated waters wash over us. But, somewhere in there in the midst of all this a seed was planted in me, a Grail question grew that had to be answered.

I viewed the film JFK later than most having spent the late 80's and early 90's drifting across America, sleeping in National Forests and elsewhere outside; "off the grid", far from movie theaters and cable television of my upbringing, I was out of the loop. Upon returning to the "real world", I finally caught the film in the mid 90's after discussing with a friend the deceptive nature of reality presented to us by mainstream views, pop culture, and media reinforced through civic mythology. I had made some sweeping generalization-as I often do-that nothing was what it seems and everything we know is wrong. My friend (Joe) quickly retorted, "Of course! I mean just look at the movie JFK for example, if we are to believe that movie…"

And that's how this all started. After my first viewing of the film the shells fell away from my eyes and my life and those closest to me were never the same…

*   *   *

I am a natural born researcher. When life presents me with a problem, I *must* solve it. And I use information to accomplish this task. The glaring moral dilemma that is the difference between the spiritual "ideals" of mainstream religious institutions of the world and their actual approach to reality applying the doctrines which form around the teachings and tenets , was a puzzle I had to solve. The crisis which arose in my own psyche being raised in a culture dominated by religious (or anti-religious) thought. The next twenty years of my life and beyond were devoted to discovering and comparing all the religions of the world and humanity, going back to their origins. I eventually came to the conclusion that there are truly thousands, millions, even billions of paths up the spiritual mountaintop. No one way excluded all others. There was no one universal religion. And if one church or temple didn't work for you, you found another, or none at all.

In the immortal last words of the Buddha: "Doubt and find your own light…"

Along the way, I discovered the lost Mysteries of the Sacred Wisdom Teachings of Humanity, something that never would have happened had I not set out on the quest for truth to begin with. Of course the fate of my immortal soul lay in balance or so I had been conditioned to believe. When I finally awoke to the significance of Fraternal Lodge systems, a subject of selective interest, with regards to the great enigma that is the United States of America and its cultural heritage, I set out once again on such a quest for truth as matters such as these of the Spirit and Psyche required, I dare say demanded, at least in myself.

For a *very* long time it seemed to me that NO ONE was interested in what is now considered the main corpus of "truther subjects" or should we say the "truther curriculum"; those subjects dealing with government conspiracies and cover-ups, false flag events, fake moon landings, dark occulted mysticism, and secret societies running amuck cavorting with aliens and trans-dimensional demons; as well as Annunaki/alien-astronaut progenitor theories, astrotheology, cryptozoology, and crypto-archeology. All these subjects, and many more unnamed sub-stream topics, clutter the chat-rooms and blog pages of the whole wide world web. More and more each day, in post-911 America, people have had the shells removed from their own eyes. People have awoken and they continue to wake up every day. They question official stories and suspect the truth is being concealed. This develops naturally in people, I think, once they start to uncover what has been covered up. "Live by the sword die by the sword…" The more you suspect, the more suspicious the world and its inhabitants become… The trick, as usual, is balance and intent.

My research into Freemasonry, and the Fraternal Lodge systems and traditions in America, was long and arduous. I approached the subject at first with skepticism and suspicion; it was an easy position to take with all the scathing bad press out there about Freemasonry and other Fraternal Esoteric Orders in general. Yet for every indicting expose, there were ten more books filled with wonder, insight, and a rich understanding of humanity that was undeniable. The dichotomy was very perplexing. When I reached the limits of understanding that my uninitiated status allowed me access to, I needed to know what actually went on in the august halls of the Lodge behind closed doors. What secrets were in fact contained therein?

My Quest remained ever vigilant, though often times tabled, or placed on the back burner, while more pressing needs demanded attention. Life goes on and we struggle, persist, and move forward. Along the way, I met my wife and we brought four wonderful children into this world. As my small family grew and the biological realization of Fatherhood gained prominence in my psyche, I once again sought to uncover within my own awareness the sort of rich tradition and cultural heritage I could bequeath to my offspring. And here again, I was struck with the stark realization of my own lack therein of true and certain mystical understanding, of context, a frame of reference to guide my children towards their own understanding and consideration of the answers to life's three great questions: Who are we? Where do we come from? Where are we going? Once again, I recognized a vacuum where the great Mystery of Western

Tradition once resided.

In life we are called to attend and engage events of fate and moments of destiny. With some events we have a choice, we can change direction, and we can switch paths and reverse the flow. Others are unavoidable-we careen towards them like a vehicle out of control and collide with them, in spite of all our best efforts to evade contact. When we are called to something by an inner passion, a divine zeal one might say, we **must** answer the call.

In 2003-4, I uncovered the lost history of my own family and discovered my mother's maternal grandfather, whom I had known until my late teens, was descended from a former POW of the English Civil war of 1650. It seems Ancestor X had been one of the sons of the Laird of Luss in Scotland and on the losing end of the Battle of September, as it was known. Placed in chains along with thousands of other prisoners, he was marched to a dungeon by the sea to await transportation to the colonies-one of Cromwell's favorite means of ethnic cleansing. After 13-odd years in the bog iron mines of Quincy, Massachusetts, Ancestor X was released into the New World to manifest his own destiny. He was eventually killed by Samoset Tribesmen near Rehoboth, Massachusetts on the eve of battle in the King Phillip's War in 1675. His son settled in my hometown, in 1690, where my family has remained ever since; though they somehow forgot their past.

Closer research of my family tree traced the roots all the way back to Scotland circa 1245 AD, when my family received the title of Laird from the Earl of Lennox. Then further back to Ireland in the 9th century during the Norse invasions of the Connach Kingdoms. My clan followed one of the Kings of Connach from Ireland into the Western Isles of Scotland-probably fleeing the Vikings. One of my ancestors became a Monk and a hermit; one of the many little islets peppering the Lochs and waterways in the region being named Monk's Isle after him; he was eventually canonized as a saint.

Tracing back through the bloodline of Knighted Lairds in my family, I found that every one of them was an initiate of one order or another. In the 14th century, just after the time of the betrayal of the original Knights Templar order by Pope Clement and King Philip the Fair-Oct. 13th 1307, one Sir John was initiated into the Order of the Grail, according to one obscure entry I found. Another Sir John, from late 16th - early 17th century, was listed as Necromancer and was, in point of fact, the last known practitioner of Black Magic and the Dark Arts in my family in

Scotland's history. He died in exile in Sicily. It was all there for anyone to find online and in a few public and private libraries and archives; a lost history of my family which ironically seemed to explain my own struggles, internally and externally, with personal destiny. This discovery awakened something in me which demanded attention.

I had been wrestling for years with a secret desire to know more about the Lodge and its inner workings. I felt drawn, albeit with a lingering skepticism, to the notion of joining a Lodge in order to know and better understand what I had gathered from my years of independent research. I seemed to understand the esoteric aspects of the Fraternal Lodge system; that beyond the charitable events and Friends of Masons cook-outs there was a secret hidden tradition spanning centuries, maybe even millennia, the motto of today's lodge being "Ancient Light in Modern Times". I had stumbled upon the notion that many were mistaken in their indictment of Esoteric Orders and the systems of spiritual development as I was beginning to understand them. I suspected that in fact many within the Lodge Systems themselves did not even realize *what* they belonged to. I would eventually find this to be true time and time again.

In the first 7 years of our marriage my wife and I moved our family 9 times, searching for a home to call our own. We settled for a time in a college town, a small city, in fact, that had become something of a "hipster mecca", a place that seemed to call us back time and again during our years of wandering. In the downtown district was the Masonic Temple, a magnificent stone building, complete with stone columns in front and a large glass window in between, with a shiny gold square and compasses and the letter "G" painted on it. Every morning, at sunrise, I would walk past this structure on my way to work in a call center and stare at the golden masonic symbol reflecting the glare of the sun rising over the downtown rooftops, and wonder what I should do. I felt called within and it grew more and more as time went by.

One particular morning, as I made my usual trek, I noticed the just-past-full moon was still visible in the West and the sun was standing just above the horizon in the East. The hermetic overtones were apparent to me; I saw myself as the 'Anthropos', the Adam Kadmon, passing between the two forces of light and darkness and right towards the porch of the Masonic temple, where the twin pillars framed the blazing symbol of the craft for my awareness to absorb. As if to drive the point home to me, at that very moment, a larger than average Red-tailed hawk flew across my path; it was my totem bird! This bird was of special significance to me as years before I drew an animal spirit card from a basket during a full moon gathering my mother brought me to. The card said, "you are a red-tailed hawk chasing the wind…" That has always stayed with me. And now this enormous hawk was flying right at the golden Square and Compass painted on the glass of the temple, talons outstretched as if seeking a perch. It squawked and shrieked as it scraped at the symbol in earnest, then finally flew to a close perch on a traffic light and stared right into my eyes, continuing to shriek. The message seemed clear to me. I was called I would join the lodge, and fulfill my Hermetic Destiny.

I travelled up the masonic ladder quickly, discovering the little known fact that once a man joins a "Blue Lodge"-as a Freemason's Lodge is called-becoming a Master Mason, he is now eligible for membership in 6-800 "concordant orders"; as in orders that predicate membership in their order on one being a member of Freemasonry. Within the first three years of my masonic career I was initiated into over 9 esoteric orders, some 20+ degrees and dubbed a Knight five times in chivalric orders by the end of five years. I joined several research bodies and gained exclusive access to both public and private collections of works and material which met my wildest expectations and beyond!

Many hours were spent with my nose buried in some ancient tome or another, much to my wife's chagrin. Finally, I had a more complete picture and understood quite clearly what was contained within the masonic corpus of teachings and instruction; especially with regards to the stewarding and guidance of several brothers within the Craft who had also discovered the truth, which we will discuss here in this book. Needless to say, I have gathered a lot of information and have a natural gift to recall and recite what I have learned, to educate those around me, whether they liked it or not, however the case may be. And my particular point of view is just twisted enough to keep many people who have been awakened to the subjects listed above interested in what I have to say.

In 2011, I was invited by internet/'new media' phenomenon Freeman Fly, of FreemanTV.com and the Freeman Perspective ongoing multi-media series, to sit in as guest host of his radio show, The Free Zone with Freeman Fly, which aired Saturday nights 8PM primetime on the now defunct Oracle Broadcasting Network out of Austin, Texas. Thousands of people follow Freeman's media worldwide after almost a decade of continuous production. Much of his research and topics of discussion were almost identical to my own. Not to mention the guests he had on which were researchers, authors and filmmakers many of which I had already reviewed in my own research! I was invited to produce and broadcast my own 2 hour live internet radio broadcast on whatever subject I wanted, with no censorship whatsoever.

The name "Frater X" was born from a quick chat between Freeman and me, trying to decide how to best present myself to the world. I liked Mr. X, or just "X", but when Freeman suggested Frater X, Latin for "Brother X", I immediately loved it. It wasn't until after we were weeks into the Free Zone broadcasts that I recalled the moniker "Frater X" had been associated with Aleister Crowley, Jack Parsons, and L Ron Hubbard. I also got a huge kick out of the synchronicity of a website dedicated to practitioners of Scientology outside the fold of the church called, that's right, "The Free Zone"!

I produced and broadcasted 8 weeks of shows on The Free Zone as guest host, inviting a close friend who took the name Jack Marshak (after the odd curator from the old 90's TV show "Friday the 13th the Series"), to join as an "embedded correspondent" from the Pacific Rim in Hilo, Hawaii. My wife assumed the moniker of Mater X, to match my "secret identity", and moderated the chat-room for the live broadcast. Many kind, and interesting, as well as intelligent listeners joined in the chat along with several thousand listeners worldwide every week. This experience changed my life forever...

When my stint on The Free Zone was coming to an end, I became anxious to continue broadcasting, believing it to be my destiny, but Oracle seemed lukewarm when I hinted around to producing a show on their network. Ironically, they seemed suspicious of me because I was a member of so many Esoteric orders-especially the Freemasons and the Knights Templar! Other radio hosts on the network were equally aloof, even openly hostile and accusatory towards me on the air live, in chat rooms and blogs; without ever even bothering to **talk** to me and get to know me. Had any even tried to do so, they could've had access to all that I had to say and the unique perspective I offered and they would have realized I meant no harm, that I only sought to educate others within and without the Lodges. But instead they attacked me, slandered me live on the air, and shunned me.

Then, on that fateful last broadcast as guest host of The Free Zone, I got a call a few hours before the show from Danny Romero-thirty year veteran of radio and then owner/executive producer of American Freedom Radio Network out of Austin, Texas. He offered me a late night Saturday slot, to which I tried to act cool as I accepted, inside I was ecstatic!

For the next three years, leading up to and including the great 2012 apocalypse swindle and afterwards, each week I provided the best two hours of internet radio I could. Reading and reviewing the material of today's cutting edge new and independent media producers and compilers, I prepared inspired and enlightening conversations, taking questions from both a chat-room, instant messages and Skype, as well as an open call line. During that time I interviewed Alan Green, the publisher of Sync Book, Volume 1-an anthology of essays on synchronicity and synchromysticism, and developed a friendship which turned into my inclusion in Sync Book, Volume 2.

And the rest, as they say, is history…

*   *   *

It is my conviction and guiding principle that I am called to serve the Order of The Mystic Tie, as I have come to think of the American Fraternity of Ancient Craft Masonry. As I put pen to paper I remain filled with hope, fervency and zeal for the Craft. It is this passion which demands this testimony of Truth that it may be known, and corrections be made and applied; that the proper course of education within Freemasonry might be restored, and countless brethren might step out from the darkness of misconception that enshrouds our august halls and lift the veil, revealing the light of certainty that Truth provides.

All Signs and portents led me to the steps of the Temple a journey which we shall begin to recount here between the covers of this book. And it shall be an epic adventure, at least I hope you think so; a voyage of discovery through the most amazing pathways, chambers, lodge halls and libraries. I have been so very fortunate to be blessed with an aptitude for the esoteric and the sacred, to be afforded access and ability to travel freely within the realms of what remains of Western Fraternal Esoteric Traditions, the Orders of Chivalry and their corresponding organizations here in America.

I was proud of and cherished my membership in these orders and would not want it thought that I intended to slander or in **any** way degrade, dishonor, or disrespect these orders. The opposite is in fact the case. I wish to clarify and even restore understanding, to the average Brother Mason and uninitiated alike, with regards to the highly misunderstood subjects of Freemasonry and Chivalric Orders specifically and occult esoteric traditions in general.

We will address the formation, establishments, and continuation of Masonic orders almost exclusively here in America by geography, constitution, and perspective; in order to bring clarity to the greater over-arching topic or question: What is the Real meaning of Masonry? What is a proper Masonic education and how might it be applied to help empower the individual freemason in the same manner as all forms of esoteric and occulted (or hidden) teachings and systems, commonly referred to as western mystery traditions? Freemasonry should rightly be considered an example of Western Mystery Tradition, in my estimation.

I approached this project with apprehension, even trepidation, rooted in the desire not to depreciate, deprecate, or otherwise diminish the image of Freemasonry proper. It is my hope that this has not happened in the material before you. Such fears had to be put aside, however, that an accurate accounting and auditing of policies and actions by individuals and groups which constitute a *secret war* (often silent and cold) within the ranks and leadership of Ancient Craft Masonry and its appendant orders-at least here in America.

A secret war which, when viewed in the context of its effects on the fraternity at large, can be seen as a microcosmic view of a still greater reality of a secret war on human consciousness, orchestrated and perpetrated against society at large, with the same genesis point in US history. And it remains my sincerest hope that the reader might view this present work as a template to apply, or overlay upon, this greater reality to which I refer within the collective social systems of the human species. Whether this goal and intention was achieved remains to be seen within the present work and by the present reader.

My introduction to Freemasonry, aside from its mysterious presence in my childhood memories and recollections as seemingly abandoned lodge structures, halls and temples peppering the New England landscape of my birth, was the news of my step-father's admission into the local Blue Lodge in my home town; I too would belong to the same nearly twenty years later, becoming the assistant secretary and assigned to write the history of the Lodge, and from which I would eventually demit or deactivate my membership. At the time of my step-father's sojourn into the Lodge, I was away at University, discovering the true realities of secondary schooling in pursuit of an utterly non-lucrative philosophy degree; a goal that would never be reached formally due to economic constraints, as well as existential limitations, though exceedingly surpassed in independent studies.

I was initially suspicious of the Lodge. Never having been one to follow the crowd, no matter my desire to be accepted and valued, I intuitively feared the secrecy and elitism I perceived emanating from behind the Lodge room doors in the inner sanctum. I was both intrigued and puzzled by my step-father's choice to join, as he was one of the few people I recognized as good, honorable and trustworthy. In order to properly understand his action and motives, I undertook a massive enterprise of studying the extensive reading, cross-referencing and researching anything and everything to do with Freemasonry and Esoteric orders in general; and included in this search was what I found regarding my own family history a long line of initiates, crusader knights and clerics, holy men and priestesses, nuns and monks.

I learned from my search that my ancestors had fought in every armed conflict in American history. From the King Phillips War to the French and Indian War, the American Revolution to the War of 1812, the War with Mexico to the Civil War, on and on and every one in between, all the way to Vietnam. My immediate family's names were all there, including my own and my mother's and my sister's, in the various web databases I consulted, such as Mormon Family Search; the Mormon's endeavor to catalog all of our bloodlines is a whole other story on its own. The more I looked, the more I found. Needleless to say I was amazed and impressed, and fundamentally influenced, by this historic and prestigious line.

It all seemed to make sense then; my interest in the esoteric, my outlook and aptitude with regards to occult philosophies, and hermetic arts. There was no doubt or question either, my path seemed obvious. I began to consider somewhat fantastical "Lovecraftian" musings of past lives and secret destinies interweaving through generations, lifetimes, and bloodlines, and wondered at the implications of such notions. My search, research and studies stepped up considerably, to the neglect and somewhat detriment of all else in my life at that time. During those years I could be found most days buried behind high stacks of old books and volumes of materials spanning the ages of humanity. I was driven, obsessed, and I could not stop.

As I have pointed out, I began my research from a suspicious slant, embracing all the bad press; even parroting to others what I now consider mostly misinformation, and/or disinformation, along with genuine chronicled accounts of the sick and twisted acts of individuals marring the image of entire groups or organizations. The more I studied the good and bad press that was being broadcast to the world, the more I became convinced that, as with many things in life, people get things wrong. At first I suspected those outside the halls of initiation were the only ones mistaken. The "profane" or uninitiated, including myself, were simply unable to understand that which we had no experiential frame of reference and therefore feared, misjudged and misconstrued what we didn't comprehend.

What I discovered when I finally entered the Temple myself and took my place among the Brethren of the Mystic Tie, was that many, if not the great majority, of those within who *had* an experiential frame of reference and symbolic instruction were just as mistaken and misinformed with regards to the true nature and meaning of Freemasonry, or Ancient Craft Masonry (its proper name), as it was originally intended and propagated here in America at least. This work is an attempt to set the records straight, correct this condition and restore Masonic Education in Freemasonry here in modern times. Enjoy!

Frater X 12/16/13

1

<u>GUARDIANS OF THE GRAIL</u>

I have always been fascinated with ancient tales of chivalry: knights and dragons, stories of magic and wizards with monsters to defeat and damsels to rescue through cunning, bravery, skill and intellect. As a child I drank deep from the wells of myth and legend. When I was young in the 1970's, my mother took a few mythology and poetry courses at the local community college where we grew up. She read me myths and epic poetry from around the world before bed each night.

Growing up I spent much of my time in bookstores and libraries. Books of fantasy and science fiction were my favorite. I was an avid player of Dungeons and Dragons often creating and leading elaborate campaigns as Dungeon Master. I was also fascinated with Trivia, fringe science and oddities, practically devouring all the Guinness Book of World Records and Ripley's Believe it or Not material I could get my curious hands on. We also owned an extensive set of World Books and Encyclopedias long before internet Google search. Combined with American pop-culture media technologies, my fertile mind took root and grew.

My parents were avid lovers of all forms of music, and we owned the only record store in our small New England Village. As my own particular brand of pattern recognition began to form, I developed questions, puzzles, and the existential riddles in consciousness of life requiring their own particular solutions. I must admit along the way I used many varieties of entheogens to explore the boundaries of these questions, with some success. Woven into my riddle of the sphinx were the three great questions asked above:

Who are we? Where do we come from? Where are we going? The next fundamentally existential question completely oversimplified is: Why?

People have spent their collective lives, energies, and potential attempting to answer these questions through various methods, approaches, beliefs, and theories.

From the Western perspective I, myself, psychically identified with Parzival, developing my own inner Grail Quest, though I did not consciously recognize it as such at first. In complete hindsight I do recognize it as such now. The more I examined the concepts and constructs of Western Myth Legend and Lore, the more I embraced them. A rich tradition of magickal arts and Hermetic occult sciences woven into fantastic tales of adventure and wonder now opened up, revealing still greater meanings and understanding of human nature, our place in Nature and the surrounding life-force; the vast active living intelligence of the Earth (nod to Phillip K. Dick).

And yet, inherently, I felt disconnected, alienated from my own nature and the greater surrounding Nature, a "stranger in a strange land". I intuitively sensed a lack of the sacred within myself, and American Society collectively, that we had devolved into a wasteland of preoccupation with consumerism and corporate greed, the industrialization of our awareness being the modern manifestation of the wasteland. For me the journey was not easy, and of course it could have been more difficult, but in the final analysis I believe we all have "our own crosses of awareness to bear", so to speak. After diagnosing my own psyche and its lack of sacred context to reality, both as an individual and part of the social collective in America and as a species, I sought a remedy.

I was naturally drawn to all things related to esoteric studies and especially the Mystery Schools. What I was discovering between the covers of all those books was that which was lost: the Great Grail Question from within the esoteric systems of Western Mystery Traditions. Things really began to take on more depth and greater dimension when I realized Freemasonry, and its Concordant Orders were among the few modern sources for contact, interaction, and instruction in said Mystery Traditions.

My entrance into the Lodge was a calculated and deliberate attempt to recapture the Western Esoteric Mystery Tradition, to take it back onboard if you will. I wanted to reignite the spark in modern contemporary consciousness, and in my own conscious-ness at the very least. I needed to fan the flame deep within the recesses of my mind back to a roaring fire of light. This is how I came to knock at the Lodge door and enter The Middle Chamber.

At the time, I working at a call center that was part of a small strip mall, the other end of which happened to be occupied by the local Masonic Organizations. It seems the Masons had let that grand stone

2

edifice (where I had my hermetic vision with the sun, moon, and hawk) slip into disrepair and beyond the point of no return, at least that was the contention of "the leadership" of the Lodge when they voted to sell the building in the late 90's for far less than its value. The hit to morale and the public image in the city is still being felt in the 21st century.

In late 2009, I found recent images posted online for an article about the building and it still looked in great shape; far better than many Lodge structures out there still in constant use. There were literally dozens of hand painted backdrops, many of which were likely oil-based, and hardwood woodworking nearly everywhere; each one a masterpiece of esoteric artwork on a full stage complete with balconies and vaulted ceiling. It was a complete and utter shame. I had no idea, when I was petitioning the lodge, *what* the real story behind that building and its loss was all about.

It is no easy task, mustering up the courage to petition a Lodge for membership and acceptance, whether you are known in the town lodge to which you apply to or not. I have done both; though, in my opinion, petitioning a lodge of strangers in an unfamiliar territory is rather more unnerving. The first stage being an unbearable wait after you give them $100 dollars (at that time, its more now) and fill out an application, to receive the mysterious light of Freemasonry. You put yourself out there for public scrutiny based on the standards of others; standards you can neither control nor affect.

After doing a basic background check, the Lodge dispatches an investigating committee to handle your petition. They make an appointment to come to your house and have a sit down with you in your living room. Then more waiting, as they report back to the Lodge of their findings and recommendation. After what seems an eternity you hear back from the Brethren, and upon acceptance an initiation is scheduled. You show up on the appointed night and time and put your life and fortune in the hands of somewhat indifferent strangers, other mortals (which has a psychic biochemical effect, all its own) then to disrobe, redress and blindfold you, the candidate, for initiation; the game is truly afoot.

The game is misdirection, one of disorientation; throwing the awareness off-balance to prepare the mind for an extraordinary, unusual allegorical and symbolic instruction. This is an important factor we must consider when approaching the systems and material contained within Western Esoteric Tradition; misdirection, deliberate distortion of perception; the deliberate and voluntary derangement of the senses in order to unpack, and take on board, information pertinent to changing consciousness.

How often in life do we actually and consciously do this? It depends on who you are, I guess. If you move around a lot, as I have, you constantly apply and reapply for housing and occupation and for this or that service or assistance. At the other end of every one of those applications is a stranger, with an indifference of varying degrees, who decides your fate based on an infinite number of probability factors. Yet something stands out as powerful and unique about approaching a Lodge, entering a stranger to those within and departing that Lodge space a friend and brother, after a remarkable spiritual transformation.

At least in philosophical theory that's how it goes. The reality is often a disappointment, without the application of a rich, inner interpretation of reality based on a greater and fuller understanding of the experience. Of course, this is the secret to true happiness and contentment in any pursuit. I considered the undertaking before me as a kind of sacred consecration; the initiation of service, not only to my own soul's growth and development, but service to my brothers within the Lodge and society at large, as well as the continued service to my family. My sacrifice on the Symbolic Altar of Freemasonry was my own "mercenary motives", to be replaced with pure and selfless intentions, and to get good results.

Having the benefit of researching my family history, and discovering a rich tradition therein, I was able to elaborate upon this in my application for the Mysteries of the Lodge. I was also asked to write a series of short articles covering my progression through the degrees, which I did, these being published in the local Scottish Rite journal. Probably more forthright than they wanted, or needed, my words were met with little response from the Brethren aside from my immediate degree coach and his cronies in the Scottish Rite, who were all too eager to recruit me into their ranks when I completed my third degree and became eligible for membership in the hundreds of concordant bodies attached to Freemasonry proper.

Initially, I was drawn to the Scottish Rite. I was operating under the idea that the various Rites within Freemasonry were formed around specific heritage as in Scottish, English, Irish, French, and German, etc., and being of Scottish descent it seemed only logical that I would join; though as it turns out, this was only partly true, in reality the "Scottish" Rite is in name only Scottish. This discovery, by the way, was a huge red flag to me that something was amiss and off kilter about this whole

Scottish Rite business. But I *was* being actively recruited and, in my ignorance, I embraced all that the brothers within the order had to offer me.

I already had a copy of Morals and Dogma, by Albert Pike, which I'd correctly determined was the textbook of the Rite. I was moved by the author's words; the sentiments and ideals resonated within me as he seemed to express an understanding of humanity's ultimate purpose couched in flowery romantic, chivalric, and strangely esoteric language which I yearned to know and understand more clearly. One particular passage spoke to me:

"Masonry should not be mere a watchtower, built upon a mystery, from which to gaze with ease upon the world, with no other result than to be a convenience for the curious. To hold the full cup of thought to thirsty lips of men; to glue to all the true ideas of Deity; to harmonize conscience with science, are the province of Philosophy. Morality is faith in full bloom. Contemplation should lead to action, and the absolute be practical; the ideal be made air and food and drink to the human mind. Wisdom is the sacred communion."   ~ Albert Pike

At the same time I was also very drawn to the Royal Arch Degree. On an intuitive level I sensed the importance in this degree, finding many cryptic messages relating to occulted esoteric meanings. I recognized something powerful in the allegorical nature of the teaching encoded within the Royal Arch Degree-and as it turns out I was correct. It became clear to me early on, that those brothers charged with supervising my instruction in the Lodge and made available for questions concerning the Craft, those assigned to my personal Masonic Education by the Master of the Lodge, seemed to know little about, nor had anything positive to say, concerning the Holy Royal Arch specifically, or the Ancient York Rite in general.

Immediately upon joining the Blue Lodge, the Lodge containing the three degrees of Freemasonry which any qualified male in any jurisdiction in America can apply for membership to, I began seeking out brethren who had "passed through the Royal Arch", as the expression goes. I did not even know this degree belonged to the degrees system within the Ancient York Rite. I was also unaware the York Rite contained the Orders of Chivalry such as the Illustrious Order of the Red Cross, the Order of Malta and the pinnacle of Freemasonry in America and the

5

Western Mysteries mythos, Knights of the Order of the Temple of Solomon or the Order of the Temple; the Knights Templar.

The brothers assigned to me-most of whom held, and still hold, prominent positions as installed officers, or simply as elder brethren-were my contacts in the Lodge. The words these brothers spoke carried the authority of the leadership of the Lodge to a new member such as myself; and who would or should know better than a 20-30 year veteran member of the Lodge? When I posed the question to the brothers assigned to me of the importance of the degrees under the jurisdiction of the York Rite to furthering a brother mason's wisdom and understanding in the Craft, as well as his spiritual growth, my queries were met with abrupt matter-of-fact statements dismissing the "need for such work", or I was given no opinion whatsoever. I was told, in no uncertain terms, that anything and everything I sought from the York Rite "…could be found within the Scottish Rite…"

As I struggled with these questions and answers, a few key individuals stepped out from the sidelines, where they toiled quietly "in the shadows of the Temple". I soon realized these brethren were the real backbone of the Lodge. They had all committed the rituals, of the Blue Lodge and the other orders of the York Rite, to "word perfect" memory long ago. They now presented a powerful and moving series of ritual degrees, polished with years of consistent working. These Sentinels of the Lodge space knew the Constitutions, Laws, and Landmarks of our august fraternity and their respective orders; having "sat" in all the chairs of office and leadership within the Blue Lodge and most other concordant orders active in the area. They had served as officers in all of the Grand York bodies as well.

These positions had many responsibilities and demanded a commitment of time and resources from each man who served, yet these brothers seemed to remain conspicuously "sidelined", as the expression goes, by the status quo obviously controlling Lodge business. Like the kid nobody picks for a pickup game of baseball, they were always assigned duties last and rarely given the task of coaching and "educating" newly made brothers. They were politically marginalized; clearly impotent when it came to leading the Lodge either through the Master's chair in the East or the Secretary's station, which is often the unofficial seat of power in any given lodge.

Tapping my shoulder, these humble servants quietly drew my attention to the truth hidden in plain sight with the three empty chairs in the East of just about every lodge room in America. There we find in the center, an obviously prominent throne-like seat, with two slightly subordinate chairs flanking it to the left and right. Yet, in all Blue Lodges, only the Master of the Lodge sits in the East; except when visiting dignitaries occasion the Lodge and are invited to join the Master. It would appear a missing triumvirate led the Lodge from the empty chairs, and in the case of the other bodies of the York Rite this is true. A three member council sits in the East presiding over the Chapter, Council, and Commandery of the York Rite.

The York Rite, in many American States, preceded the formation of Grand governing bodies in their jurisdictions. Hence these State Grand Lodges had to request and receive their power and authority from the members of preexistent Rites, Orders and subordinate bodies. Nowadays these Grand Lodges dispense their authority and approvals from some misguided sense of authority over these same concordant orders and rites that initially approved their formation.

Equally remarkable to me were the assertions made by these Guardians of Truth, that Ancient Craft Masonry in America was, in point of fact, a dynamic spiritual and educational system that instructed each brother Mason according to his aptitude and merit, on the "Secret Arts and Divine Sciences of the Soul". They told me that Ancient Craft Masonry was in fact a complete system of ceremonial and ritual instruction, contained within all the York Rite Orders of Freemasonry-which included the Blue Lodge degrees! The Blue Lodge was, in fact, the first Order of the four bodies of the York Rite, which also included The Royal Arch Chapter, The Cryptic Council and The Orders of Chivalry in the Commandery.

The most potent of their assertions and contentions was the bold accusation leveled against the most powerful and wealthy Order attached to Freemasonry proper: the (so-called) Ancient and Accepted Scottish Rite! The charges made by the Guardians of the Grail, who had taken me under their wing, were that the Scottish Rite was not only fraudulent in its claims of authority and Templar lineage, and was in fact not Freemasonry at all; but also that the bodies and degrees of the Scottish Rite amounted to nothing more than an impetuous and relatively modern contrivance, an innovation foisted upon Freemasonry as some legitimate companion to our order.

This all stood in stark contrast to the assertions of elder brothers in the Lodge, known to me as members of both Rites and assigned to instruct me in the Craft, who went so far as to say that if they had it to do over again, they would not have joined the York Rite! My only recourse was to investigate the roots of both the York Rite and the Scottish Rite, and the origin of this obvious power struggle; this secret cold war waging on almost imperceptibly for decades, even centuries.

And all the while, statements about Freemasonry like this one from the Oklahoma York Rite website, reminded me of a bigger picture at play:

"It almost seems magical to realize that when we took our obligations at the Altar of Masonry, we entered into a shared covenant with untold generations of men who had the same aspirations of brotherhood; the same longing for self-improvement. In Masonry, we call this *The Mystic Tie*. This Mystic Tie happens also to be one of the most important reasons why Master Masons choose to join the higher bodies of Masonry. The many lessons of virtue, morality, ethics, religion and spirituality taught in Masonry are vast and require many levels of instruction."

So, it seems my course was set. I began by focusing the might of my ability to gather and process information on one of the most curious trivial and almost inexplicably powerful and wealthy Rites the world has ever known...

2

THE BIRTH OF THE SCOTTISH RITE

" The Ancient and Accepted Scottish Rite is neither wholly European nor wholly American...and it is particularly important to observe that the rituals were almost completely rewritten by Albert Pike and that it was American organizational ability which gave it the body and stability necessary for a world-wide system..."

~Henry W. Coil Sr., Freemasonry through Six Centuries Vol. 2 Chapter 10 (1968)

The fraternal organization known as the Ancient and Accepted Scottish Rite is "neither wholly American nor wholly European", as Coil tells us above. It is very important to observe that the rituals contained within this order have been completely reworked and rewritten, over and over again, more times than is humanly possible to count, and not just by Albert Pike. In true fact, Scottish Rite "Valleys", as any city or town jurisdiction is referred to, allow their active members to rewrite and rework the 32-odd rituals of the order to meet the needs and prerogatives of local "Lodges of Perfection", quietly invoking the Bavarian Illuminati's Perfectibilis Grade of that degree system. This practice, by brothers "old" and new, provides an almost complete breakdown of continuity with regards to maintaining true tradition.

"Freemasonry through Six Centuries", by Henry W. Coil, is an inspiring and exhaustive work, the title of which is telling as to the origins and timeline of Ancient Craft Masonry in the world. At the opening of Chapter 10, Vol. 2, Brother Coil (whom we will be discussing more in pages to come) goes on to describe the development of the various degrees and rites in the "Continental" (or European) degree systems of the 18th century and how a wholly new innovation called the "Ancient and Accepted Scottish Rite", or simply the Scottish Rite, grew out of a product of these Continental Degree Systems as a transplantation of something called the "Rite of Perfection"; a hybrid of French and German quasi-Templar Grades originally containing 25 degrees.

Coil reiterates that the Ancient Craft Masonry method found in the York Rite is more traditional. The method of delivery and instruction is as close to exactly as it has always been. It mirrors the Blue Lodge three degree system as well, where the entrant (candidate) is conducted through the Lodge, having degrees communicated to him personally as an active participant in ceremonies consisting of lectures, floor work, and charges in an unbroken tradition where companion masons were and are made. Lodges, Chapters, and Councils were formed and ceremonies were performed in order to continue to initiate new entrants.

He informs us that this method was deemed unnecessary to the Continental Systems, which the "Americanized" Scottish Rite inherited in the Continental and subsequent Scottish Rite systems, where these degrees and titles were and are still, regarded as something that could simply be passed along to others by "patent"; like a deed conveying title to real and actual property. These could be freely given out, by anyone else holding such a patent, that they too might pass on the rights and titles to others still. Under such a system, thousands of degree holders were created who had never even seen the interior of a real Freemasons Lodge. How full or how scant the explanation and exposition of the degrees, was a matter of choice and judgment to the patent holder transmitting the degrees and patents; whereby the process might continue to proliferate indefinitely throughout Freemasonry in America and the world!

An ornate and prestigious looking document, with a stunning gold seal and archaic symbols and exotic languages, the patent letter, like an official government document or license today, proves its validity in itself and could not really be disputed especially in the eyes of the average Master Mason of any given Lodge in 19th century America. And so, a new authority was established, riding concurrent with the traditional Ancient Craft Masonry system. And from this arose the confusion, distortions-and disturbances which characterize the history, first of the Continental Degree Systems of France and Germany, and then the American Systems of Freemasonry.

The pitch was so persuasive really to any man of that era; to possess for themselves 32 pseudo-prestigious princely and honorable titles, all at the cost of a maybe half a month's pay at the most, or maybe even free, and one day or evening's worth of time. This would be a big seller to any man of that era, and indeed in our own, where time truly had become a priceless commodity. And it sold over and over again from sea to shining sea.

The birth of the Scottish Rite in America was midwifed by one such patent as described above, issued by authorities Freemasonic in nature, in France sometime in the mid-18th century. This really is the best way to describe it. Following the tidal shift of allegiance between French and English Masons, with the French declaration of Independence, the French Grand Lodge System embraced the more Jacobite "Scots Masters" Lodge, which effectively distanced them from the Grand Lodge of England. Of course, the strife between these two nations and their peoples goes without saying, and stretches back to the early roots of both societies.

Returning to the timeline, it seems a patent was presumably issued to one Stephen Morin, August 27th 1761 and it purported to grant to Morin, who is described as "...Grand Perfect Prince of All Orders of Masonry of Perfection, Member of the Royal Lodge of Trinity...under title of Lodge of St. John and surnamed Perfect Harmony", the Right to form and establish a Lodge in order to admit to and multiply the Royal Order of Masons in all the Perfect and Sublime Degrees. The patent further authorized him to "...govern the members and choose the Officers, to reform the observance of the Laws of the Order, to create Inspectors..." and it constituted him "Grand Master Inspector to establish Perfect and Sublime Masonry in all parts of the world."

There was apparently some difficulty discerning what body or bodies issued the patent, or what their authority was, and from where it issued forth. It seems a list of 25 degrees was attached to the supposed copy of this patent found by Coil in Charleston, South Carolina, the assumed headquarters of the SR Supreme Council, over which degrees the Council of the Emperors of the East and West (the governing body from France at that time in the 18th century) held exclusive authority and control.

The patent does seem to be confined to the degrees "above" the three degrees of the Blue Lodge and he reports it has evidently always been interpreted as such. And so from this we have the transplanting of a group of degrees, under a supposed Rite of Perfection, granting extraordinary powers and unjustifiable blanket authority over all the orders of Masonry to a Stephen Morin, from an unknown authority and equally unknown source, growing into something entirely different which we now refer to as the Scottish Rite.

And now a word about "Rites"; here is what the Indiana Cryptic Monitor of Freemasonry states, "Our word 'rite' comes directly from the Latin and perhaps goes back to Sanskrit 'riti' meaning a stream or a running way or 'ri', denoting flow". Webster's dictionary, among other definitions, gives the following: "...the act of performing divine or solemn services as established by law, precept, or example; a format, act or series

11

of acts of religion or solemn duty; a solemn observance." The word ritual likewise comes from the same root, the ritual being the customary way in which history and tradition are portrayed and their lessons taught. Going back to the primary meaning of the word, it is the equivalent in meaning to the word "ceremony". Hence, Masons use it in the context of following a fixed trend, or channel, a customary way of doing things. Consider these definitions and meanings when we refer to rites, rituals, ceremonies, etc.

Even though Robert Gould's six volume History of Freemasonry (1889) is obviously in support and favor of the Scottish Rite, with many high ranking 33rd degree authoring essays in the revised editions, therein we still find remarkable critiques and assessments of this enigmatic order's origins. Robert Folger, a well-known and very outspoken critic of the Scottish Rite and the Supreme Council wrote an expose called "The Ancient and Accepted Scottish Rite in 33 Degrees" (1881), which is footnoted as such in Volume 4 of Gould's History. "They [the Scottish Rite degrees] are simply modern trash (Pike's own assessment of the degrees he received from Mackey!), without a single feature or quality in them which would recommend them to the favorable consideration of worthy and sensible brethren. This is the opinion of which we entertain now and have entertained for long years concerning these degrees..."[1]

He goes onto discuss the establishment of Ancient Craft Masonry in America, telling us the rituals in the old Grand Lodge systems in America (excepting perhaps Pennsylvania) have been revised and rewritten many times over as were the English originals.[2] He states that many of the ceremonies now in use in America, which are regarded as "Landmarks" in the ritual, were innovations of two renowned masonic lecturers and ritualists, Thomas Smith Webb and his Most Illustrious successor Jeremy L. Cross; whom we will examine further in pages ahead. It seems clear from this that the Craft Degrees did, in fact, evolve over time into what we have today. A close, comparative study of the history of the degrees confirms this. We know the Royal Arch Degree was being worked as early as the 1740's. D'Assigny mentions it first in Dublin, in 1744, and that soon after that the Knight Templar Degree was being given in England and Ireland; though it is presumed these had already being given in Scotland even earlier.

In fact, with the creation of a three degree system in Craft Masonry and the Royal Arch and Knight Templar, degree-making in the British Isles came to an end for a very long time. The Knights of the Rose Croix (Cross) and Kadosh manifested eventually under the auspices and authority of the Grand Prior of Knights Templar in England until the early 1830's, when the United Kingdom finally opened the doors of Craft Masonry to the so-called higher degrees. Among those was the Ancient and Accepted Rite (the Anglican version of the Scottish Rite) who obviously pressured the Templars of England to surrender the Kadosh and Rose Croix degrees, holding sway over them in the rest of the world. But in the mid-1700s, there were no other higher degrees allowed in England. Instead the enterprise of "degree-making" spread throughout the Continent of Europe from the edge of the Sea inward, these degrees and their authors proliferating a tidal surge of degree inventors with claims that their degrees were higher than the Craft degrees!

This so-called "Higher Grade" masonry took root and flourished with great vigor in France and also in Germany. The numerous "inventors" would roam the Continent peddling their custom made degrees, attaching absurd lineages and imposing mythic histories to these "Haute Grades". They contained nonsensically transparent historical anachronisms "…Too contemptible for consider…" according to Gould. [3] Not to mention the pseudo-Scotch Masonic fantastical geographic claim of the Myth of Heredom mountain which is at the root of many of these quasi-Templar grades and degrees. In France, the making of Masonic high grades was a thriving business for about 50 years after the introduction of Craft Masonry there in 1725, during which hundreds of so-called "masonic" degrees were produced and hawked everywhere but the UK.

Let us now consider the implications of this. The system which we call Ancient Craft Masonry evolved from a three degree system plus the Royal Arch and Knight Templar degrees that were all modified from an extant one degree "operative" system in the region of the British Isles, along with other various sources to be discussed. Said Craft Masonry, migrating to France and the Continent in the early 18th century, was seized upon with great fervor, inspiring the explosive propagation of hundreds of imitation degrees all claiming affinity and authority derived from their supposed connection to Ancient Craft Masonry; even though we know these inventors were literally peddling these extravagant claims and degrees for profit! It is from this playing field that we discover the origins of the Scottish Rite.

A man known as Chevalier Bonneville is said to have constituted a chapter in Claremont, France, in 1754, which was called the Rite of Perfection, or Rite of Heredom, and contained within it 25 degrees. [4] Also included in this list of 25 were the first 3 Craft Degrees of the Blue Lodge, a 13th degree called the Royal Arch, as well as an 18th degree called the Knight of the Rose Croix (cross). According to Gould, all 25 of the degrees listed had been floating around France detached from each other for many years. In 1759 the Council of the Emperors of the East and West organized in Paris under this Rite, or system of degrees, also consisting of 25 degrees-virtually the same degrees as Bonneville's Rite of Perfection; and this new *Council of Emperors* began conferring the 1st three degrees of the Blue or Symbolic Lodges in 1761.

At the beginning of Chapter 42 of Gould's History of Freemasonry, titled "The Introduction of the Rite of Perfection in America", it is explained that the Royal Arch Degree was practiced in America as early as 1758, and the Knight Templar degree from 1769. Gould informs us the establishment and rise of the Council of Emperors of East and West, containing the same 25 degrees of the Rite of Perfection, persisted in France "...down to a period when their History was lost in the general wreck of matter that took place in France in the latter part of the 18th century..."; which leaves us with a fog of uncertainty with regards to the circumstances surrounding the creation of the Morin Patent, a truly unique one of a kind document.[6]

Stephen Morin was granted power through his patent which, it would seem, was issued by this Council of Emperors. Something called a "facsimile of the Patent of the Lodge of Perfection Albany, NY 1767" is referred to in the text of the chapter as a "translation" from the original French document; current whereabouts unknown, validity unconfirmed, and of questionable authority.[5] Though the essayist in Gould's History is quick to state that the Morin Patent is beyond reproach for its authenticity, we remain unconvinced. As we have seen and will continue to uncover, the years in question and the true origins and purposes of these Councils and Orders are lost to history. It all seems very dubious.

Nonetheless, pressing onwards and putting this uncertainty aside, we go on to learn that Morin arrives on the Island of San Domingo sometime in the latter part of 1761 or early 1762 according to most accounts on the subject. It is here that we are told he establishes a Council of Princes of the Royal Secret and subsequently a Grand Orient for High Grades in the New World. He also establishes a Council of Princes in Kingston, Jamaica in 1770. The Rite remained "offshore", in Morin's hands, until at least 1767, and it seems that he was in the Caribbean for over ten years. Speculating from the text cited from the "Historical Inquiry" into the Grand Constitutions of 1786 by Brother Albert Pike (whom we will discuss further in the next few chapters) clearly admits "...at what date we do not find...", with regards to when Morin made one Andrew Francken an Inspector General. Francken is a key player in this timeline. [7]

It would seem more probable that it was, in fact, Francken who propagated the degrees of the Rite to the North American Continent, as Francken is reported to have communicated the Rite of Perfection to one Moses M. Hays in Boston; though once again there is question in regards to the dates. Brother Hays is supposed to have communicated the Rite to one Barend M. Spitzer, in Charleston, though no date is given. One problem with this is that Brother Spitzer's authority is supposedly derived from a patent issued at the Convention of Inspectors in Philadelphia 1781, which he uses to communicate and empower one John Mitchell Deputy Inspector General. It is all very convoluted and unclear, to say the least.

Keep in mind that the most important aspect of all this, for the purpose of this book, is that all of these references to the Rite being "communicated", a practice that has continued up to the present day, is a very broad, sliding scale of standards, most assuredly inconsistent and incomplete. There was no standardized practice or approach in this regard; all was left to the peddler of the degrees and rites, as had been the prevailing tradition in France for half a century. Gould's final word on the Morin Patent identifies it as probably the first (pseudo) Masonic document of its kind issued.

The Morin Patent is described as a hallmark of the beginning of one of the greatest abuses with which Freemasonry has been afflicted; "...the placing of almost limitless legislative, executive, and administrative Masonic powers in the hands of irresponsible individuals, who too often used their authority for mercenary purposes and to sub serve their own selfish ends, has been the cause of endless trouble to honest honorable High Grade Masonry. Any one of them (Inspector Generals) clothed with the authority of a patent as a Deputy Inspector General could and most of them did, roam over the countryside conferring degrees, and creating still more Inspector Generals at their pleasure for a pecuniary consideration, seldom for love or affection-either for their victims, or for the Order..." [8]

An interesting and telling assessment of the early founders of the so-called Rite of Perfection, which as we know would later become the Scottish Rite, a pseudo-Masonic order, in that the claims are made in name only to lineage tracing back to the establishment of English Craft Masonry in France, in 1725; not to mention the boastful claims to Templar lineage. We can clearly see, and have shown, a distinct break within Craft Masonry occurred in French and so-called Continental Masonry when innovations, such as the hundreds of extra-numerary degrees, were accepted and modifications allowed, with impunity, by individuals with no real or true authority to do so. These modifications to the rites and degrees in France and the Continent produced something other than traditional Ancient Craft Masonry. Hence the policy of irregular status between the Grand Orient of France (the body recognized as having authority over Freemasonry in that country) and the Grand Lodges of Ancient Craft Masonry in England and America, especially, which remains to this day.

To clarify, many higher grades or degree systems have and do exhibit a number of novel themes and elaborations which travel away from the prevailing theme within Ancient Craft Masonry; it is this author's contention that certain modifications serve to reinforce exemplification of themes, lessons and teachings, such as the idea of a Knight Mason laboring in the Temple ruins with trowel in one hand and sword in the other, searching and exploring the ancient vaults, crypts, underground archways and workings of the Holy City for that which is lost...

Coil tells us the "Scots Master", or Cryptic Degree, was modified from this imagery "...discovered usually in the 9th Arch, the long lost Master's Word (lost and not found in the Master Mason Degree, but substituted) the most profound and ultimate secret in Freemasonry hitherto unknown to the common craft its place having been filled by a substitute. This word was the ineffable name of Deity and the degrees embracing this idea were called Cryptic or Ineffable..." He goes on to say the group of degrees embracing this might be called "Arch Masonry. [9]

I would like to point out that what is clear in the "American Rite", or Ancient Craft Masonry proper, is that the lost word is found and restored in the Royal Arch Degree! Hence Coil's desire to allude to "arches". We shall see the Royal Arch and the ineffable aspect of this theme throughout the Scottish Rite system and we will continue to examine what seems to be a deliberate rationalization and coopting of similarity that is truly forced, given many realities. The Scottish Rite, it seems, amounts to a foreign and irregular modification of Freemasonic themes which move the body of the work within the Scottish Rite far beyond the traditions of the Craft as propagated first in the British Isles and then America.

The Scots Masters mentioned above were the predecessors to the high ranking (33rd degree) Scottish Rite Masons of today. Since the Scots Masters possessed the secrets of their own degree, they were deemed to be of higher rank than "ordinary" masons. They claimed to out-rank all others, even when visitors to another Lodge. They even wore distinct clothing from other masons. According to Coil, the Scots Masters claimed the right to personally impart the secrets of the three degrees of the Blue Lodge to anyone without ceremony, at their will and pleasure! And that Scots Masters' conduct could only be called into question by other Scots Masters; a clear pattern of "elite control" for the benefit of the few at the expense of the many. [10]

The Grand Lodges of both France and Germany were at times under the direct control of Scots Masters or Scots Directories. What remains so very remarkable about this all is the Templar Chivalric Doctrine, which as Coil himself states on page 286 of Vol. 1, "...departs markedly and in almost every way from that of Craft Masonry, which descended from the Operative Masons who were workmen, Tradesmen, or Artisans...an entirely different stratum of society from the Princes, Dukes, Counts, Earls, and Knights who formed the ruling and warrior class of feudalism...". So by the very claims of so-called High Grade Masonry to any connection with the original Templar-Chivalric Tradition, it is truly separated from Craft Masonry.

In fact, tracing the development and propagation of the Rite of Perfection to its later incarnation, the Scottish Rite, and throughout world history, we find a pattern of ideological dispute in nation after nation always drawn down the lines of Papal or Ecclesiastical Monarchy or fascist state control on one side and a Populist Democratic Republicanism on the other. Invariably I found that, throughout the 18th and 19th centuries, The Scottish Rite was on the side of "the Cross and Crown" of Rome and King, not the true and actual Templarism. This was just as often the case in the Democratic Republican Populist camp, as in the specific case of Mexico in the years leading up to its own Revolutionary Civil War in the early 19th century, which we will examine.

Returning now to the formation of the Scottish Rite in the New World, and to Henry Coil, where he too describes the lawless chaos and flagrant abuses of power and prestige which characterized the propagation of the Scottish Rite, and its own "founding fathers" in early America.

"...The chief invention of the French, the idea that the degrees and orders could be transferred and transmitted by patent or virtually a power of attorney. By the magic word or touch of one holding such authority any number of individuals, even complete [unqualified] strangers might be endowed with degrees from the lowest to the highest on sight and irrespective of instruction in the tenets or precepts of those degrees or Freemasonry in general, that depended entirely on the patent holder...In this manner degrees and titles became more glittering baubles, the recipient of which was not one whit more instructed than he was before; though he bore the most resplendent Princely titles of dignity and preeminence. Moreover, the newly endowed brother could be vested with power to pass these titles along to others." [11]

He goes on to say that the patent of Stephen Morin is one of a kind, and reiterates, that while Morin's Patent was responsible for bringing the Rite to America, and morphing into an orderly system, it also furnished precedence for conflict and trouble in America, and France alike, for years to come. Brother Coil also explains how the patent system employed by the Scottish Rite was not adopted by the York, even in the Higher Grades and Orders, continuing instead to embrace the operative ideal of the Masonic Lodge, truly symbolizing the ancient meeting places of workmen, "as Brothers for mutual aid and instruction"; while the York Rite continues to personally conduct initiation or instruction in ceremonies in which the Candidates and Officers participate and other members observe.

The American Rite did have its degree peddlers according to Coil, a practice that was made easy and profitable by the thirst for degrees or titles which seems always to have been an aspect of the Craft. The distinction made of the "extra-numerary" York degree peddlers was that they were always done as side degrees, and they never resulted in any schisms and did little if any harm.

Shifting our focus once again to another source of research, The History of the Ancient and Honorable Fraternity of Free and Accepted Masons and Concordant Orders, revised by a board of editors in 1926 from a work copy written by Lee C. Hascall, cites the Revolution as the origin point of the American Rite, and in throwing off allegiance with England, and following the U.S. establishment of independence, "...the ritual of the fraternity was made distinctly American by the blending of the Ancients and Moderns of England (two significantly differing approaches to Craft Masonry)...with that of Scotland and Ireland and as then revised and pruned of its surplus." [12]

The particular series of degrees we keep referring to as the American System has framed all the relevant pieces of the various traditions and themes into a superstructure of conception. The symbolic degrees of the Blue Lodge, the sacred work commenced but unfinished, along with the Chapter or Capitular Degrees of the Royal Arch and the Cryptic Degrees, supply the essential substitution material to finish the structure of the abode of the Divine. The blending of the Orders contained within the York Rite-especially the first three: Symbolic, Capitular, and Cryptic-provide all the appliances, furniture, and ornamentation necessary to understand the Temple structure in this context.

Moving forward, we are told that the outgrowth of "the American scion of Ancient Craft Masonry" could be said to bear little resemblance to the British parent stock and that "the work of the Ancients and Moderns in England and the work of the Continental Rites came to this country about the same time…they were inter-blended to such an extent that from a ritualistic point of view, a new Masonry may be said to have been created…Webb and his associates made, out of the conglomeration of work, a new work which was afterwards embellished by Cross and others, and very generally received is now the foundation upon which our rituals are built." [13, 14]

In 1791, a revolution commenced in San Domingo, exactly 30 years after Stephen Morin established the New World Rite of Perfection there. France lost its rule of San Domingo in 1802, and Morin's Supreme Council body ceased to exist there, returning to Paris and forming a new Supreme Council in France with French Scots Masons, fusing the Scottish Rite of Heredom with the Ancient and Accepted Rite of Perfection. Eventually the Supreme Council was absorbed by the Grand Orient of France, though it maintained open warfare until 1862, furthering the long held controversy that it was known to care more about increasing its own powerbase than really propagating Craft Masonry.

Hascall gives the final assessment of the Grand Orient, the ruling Masonic body of France, on page 804; "…in changing its Constitutions so as to admit atheists… (The Grand Orient) has violated the fundamental principle in Freemasonry [belief in Deity] and ceased to be a Masonic body." In regards to the history of the Southern Jurisdiction of the Supreme Council in America, we are told (on page 806) that it is "a record of controversies exceedingly bitter; the energies of the members of its obedience were expended in disputes, to the sacrifice of the propagation of the Rite. Then came the Anti-Masonic craze and the Rite was nearly swept out of existence. Its records were almost lost and nearly all its archives shared the same fate…"

So far endangered was the Rite of Perfection in America that Thomas Webb, in his 1805 edition of Illustrations of Freemasonry Part Two, titled The Ineffable Degrees, prefaced as such: "...the general design of this part of the work is to preserve the History and charges of the several Ineffable Degrees from falling into oblivion (!) with which they have long been threatened, as well as from the small number of conventions of Masons who possess them, as from the little attention that has been paid to their meetings of late years(1797)".

And so we find the newly transplanted Rite of Perfection barely functioning as the 18th century closes. The Revolution in America allowed for Continental Degrees of many various Grand Lodge Systems to slide under the doorway of Ancient Craft Masonry and into the formation of many new American Grand Lodge Systems, working tirelessly to consolidate power and prepare for an historic opportunity. Meanwhile, the York Rite formed out of a blend of various traditions of Ancient Craft Masonry that also grafted itself to America, during its Colonial Period. The York Rite of America became the Nation's established mainstream tradition of Craft Masonry, firmly rooted in the independence of the Nation and strengthened by its Ancient Landmarks and Traditions. The Rite of Perfection seemed to have experienced early growth at the beginning of 18th century; in America, it all but imploded by century's end.

The York Rite was clearly known, born, and based in America, in its present form since the Revolution, as the American Rite. The Rite of Perfection was introduced into America by Francken, one in a long line of degree peddlers, and it was understood by those practicing that the Supreme Council and governing bodies were, in fact, based first in Berlin, and then in Paris.

After the early years of the 19th century, the Rite of Perfection enters a confusing period of semi-dormancy leading up to the early years before the Civil War in America, when it fully reorganized under the authorship and vision of Albert Pike, as Grand Commander, from an almost defunct "...pile of rubbish...", as Pike would describe the loose-leaf stack of hand-written degrees. Legend has it the famous Masonic scholar, Dr. Albert Mackey, communicated the Rite to Brother Pike.

This journey we have taken, through the early years and history of the Rite of Perfection in Europe and America has been saturated with so many unsubstantiated claims, with no clear or valid documentation to prove any of them. Over and over again, precise terms, empowerments, and dates of this or that document or Council body cannot be ascertained with anything like absolute certainty, or even probability. One would expect an Order with such dubious origins and histories to fade away and cave in on its own house of false cards, as is how we find the Rite at the turn of the 19th century. And yet, somehow this was not to be the end of the Rite of Perfection. Somehow the body would rally and become in fact the largest, richest and most influential of all the Rites and Orders attached to Freemasonry, travelling all the way to the Moon!

In the next chapter we will consider a key operative and the one man, if any, whose influence and skills may account for the drastic changes and success of such a strange and obscure group of degrees and traditions.

3

THE MERLIN OF MASONRY

Between 3rd and 4th Street on D Street NW, between the Department of Labor Building and the Municipal Building in Washington DC, stands an eleven foot tall bronze likeness of a man who was not only the only Confederate Military Officer or figure to be honored as such (he held the rank of Brigadier General and was yet, in fact, found guilty of Treason), but also who had more impact than any other individual on Ancient Craft Masonry worldwide, especially in America, aside from perhaps the infamous Captain William Morgan.

Dedicated Oct. 23rd 1901, by a resolution in Congress 1898; due in large part to the efforts of two prominent Scottish Rite members of Congress, Congressman James D Richardson 33rd Degree from Tennessee and Senator Henry M. Teller 33rd Degree from Colorado; the statue was originally erected in front of the House of the Temple (official headquarters of the Scottish Rite Supreme Council 33rd Degree) in Washington, D.C. later moved in 1977, for reasons unknown, to its present location.

It may not seem remarkable to many that this statue exists. Most would probably assume he simply had some profound impact on Government and society at large in America. And they would be right. What might not be assumed, or even suspected, is that this statue is the only one standing in Washington, D.C. that is memorializing a convicted war criminal; he was found guilty of treason for fighting on the side of the Confederacy during the Civil War, not to mention misconduct on the battlefield; and for his involvement in the conspiracy of Lincoln's assassination(!). He was pardoned shortly thereafter by newly-minted President Andrew Johnson. Johnson yielded under pressure from constituents, in exchange for the President's being made a 32nd degree Prince of the Royal Secret; this following a meeting with high-ranking Official Representatives from the Supreme Council, in his bedroom, in the White House.

Who was this obviously well-connected and influential man? One quick search on the internet will reveal literally millions of opinions answering this question. And, as with all controversial and historic figures, it is nearly impossible to reconstruct a clear and accurate picture whilst wading through such a sea of speculations. But in this chapter, we shall attempt just that; using as a guiding principle, the desire to focus almost exclusively on aspects of his life and career which bring clarity and understanding to the main thesis I am advancing here.

We are speaking, of course, of the infamous Albert Pike. I will not attempt to revise or retell the biography of Brother Pike beyond the most basic and generally accepted information. There are sufficient biographical materials available for further review, to give a clear enough portrait of the man's beginnings and background. First let us look at where the rubber meets the road, virtually speaking. For instance, the website dcpages.com offers an interesting series of photos and text commentary emphasizing the bronze statue in D.C. of General Pike.

One of the first things we learn looking at the site, is that Albert Pike "...was "the Head of the Masonic Fraternity"; a spurious and suspicious claim to say the least, completely unsubstantiated if we are to consider the man based on his rank as leader of the Scottish Rite, which is not of Freemasonry but has *attached* itself to Freemasonry! Nonetheless, the boastful, inaccurate claim is made. Another photo in the series on the site, titled "Pike stands above a god", depicts the statue with a bronze female likeness at his feet. We are told in the commentary that this represents Athena, named there as the "Goddess of Freemasonry", with a quote from the Pagan Mithraic Mysteries as proof text! I do not personally recall hearing, at any point, any such reference to Athena as specifically Goddess of *anything* in Freemasonry, or even being mentioned anywhere in the official Rituals, Lectures, and Floor Work of Ancient Craft Masonry in America.

We are told that Edgar Allan Poe praised Pike as one of America's greatest Classical Poets; the site then quoting a redundant Confederate Nationalistic verse by the man. The Mysteries of Isis and Osiris are mentioned, as well as the suggestion that Pike was not only "Masonry's Merlin", but also a modern-day Plato, Homer and Zoroaster; telling us that he was thought of as such in his own time.

Born in Boston, Massachusetts in 1809, Pike spent his childhood in the picturesque colonial fishing village of Newbury-port, north of Boston, and also in Framingham, where he remained until he was 15. He passed his entrance exams and was accepted at Harvard in 1825, though when the University requested 2 years tuition in advance, he chose not to attend. He became a school teacher, first in Gloucester and later in North Bedford,

Fairhaven, and Newburyport. Another version of his Harvard career says he attended one year and doubled up his course study load, passing the exams for both first and second year, but when the University demanded payment for two years-worth of tuition anyway, he withdrew never to return and complete his studies. In 1859 he received an Honorary PhD from Harvard but declined it.

Albert Pike's travel years are the stuff of legends. In many ways, and by many accounts, he was larger than life, not the least of which was his physical stature; standing over six feet tall, he had a wide girth, with a dark, and eventually grey, mane of long hair flowing down to his shoulders. Many legends and myths seemed to have followed this man in his own lifetime.

After 1831, Pike travelled west. Living in Missouri for a time he joined an expedition to Taos, New Mexico, and at some point during which Pike was separated from his horse, and left to walk the remaining 500 miles to Taos. He went on to Texas travelling a circuit of 1300 miles, 650 on them on foot, and eventually settled in Arkansas in 1833.

He wrote a series of articles for the Arkansas Advocate, under the penname "Casca"; with the series' popularity earning him a permanent position on the paper, by 1835 Pike was sole owner the Advocate, promoting the Whig Party political view-points as such. Supposedly teaching himself Law by studying the Complete Set of Roman Law, he was admitted to the Bar in 1837, selling the Advocate that same year. He was the first reporter for the Arkansas Supreme Court, and also wrote a book (published anonymously) titled: The Arkansas Form Book, which was a guide for lawyers. A true renaissance man, he studied spoke and wrote upon many subjects, legal or otherwise. He produced highly regarded poetry in his day, with several volumes of his mostly forgotten works published, posthumously, by his daughter.

Up to the Civil War, Pike seems to have manifested a rather affluent lifestyle as legal counsel to several Native Tribes, includ-ing the Choctaw Nation of Oklahoma, who signed a favorable Treaty with General Pike in 1861. He would inevitably enter the war on the side of South, serving as Brigadier General of the Confederacy commanding Indian forces. For his efforts to defend Dixie, Pike was ruined financially, leaving him impoverished for the rest of his life, often borrowing money for basic living ex-penses from the Supreme Council, before the Council voted him a lifetime annuity of $1,200 in 1879, which he received each year until his death in 1891.

Later in life he would winter in Washington, D.C. and spend his summers on the frontier, encamped in Indian Territory. It seems General Pike was the life of the party in the D.C. social circles he frequented. He was an imposing figure, known to speak several languages and well-versed in many extraordinary systems of knowledge and wisdom, as well as esoteric symbolic secrets and traditions. He seems to have thrilled and delighted the ladies of high society, with amazing orations and accounts of intrigue and adventure. Once while on expedition in Indian Territory, as he of-ten was in the summer, word went back to D.C. that General Pike had expired. As a response to this news, there was organized an elaborate funeral procession and memorial service, which Pike promptly attended, and gleefully imbibed, celebrating the exaggerated news of his demise!

Such was the man it seems. While in Arkansas, before the war in the 1840's, Pike joined an Independent Order of Odd Fellows Lodge; rising rapidly to attain the chair of "Noble Grand", the presiding office. After joining the Odd Fellows Lodge, Pike entered the Blue Lodge of American Craft Masonry, joining Western Star Lodge #2 in Little Rock, Arkansas, in 1850. On November 4th, 1852, he demitted from Western Star and affiliated with Magnolia Lodge #60, of Little Rock, serving as Master of the Lodge (also a charter member) in 1853. He demitted from Magnolia, then re-affiliated, in 1854 and remained a member until his death. In 1858, he affiliated with Marion Lodge #68, of New Orleans, Louisiana; demitting in 1860. He was made an honorary member of Kilwinning Lodge #341 Memphis, Tennessee, February 24, 1871. He later affiliated with Pentalpha Lodge #23, of Washington, D.C. in 1880, and demitted 1883.

One interesting fact about Pike's various Masonic member-ships is that he was a High-ranking York Rite Mason, as well. Exalted to the Sublime Degree of the Holy Royal Arch in 1850, he joined the Cryptic Council in 1852, and the Templar Commandery in 1853; a month after joining the Commandery, he received the 4-32 Degrees of the Scottish Rite from Albert Mackey, as a stack of loose leaf handwritten papers. The Scottish Rite really began its meteoric rise to prominence after this time. It is important to state, for the sake of this discussion, that we will never know-even with the propensity of documentary material and citation evidence, no matter how conflicting-what truly motivated this influential man, nor the extent of the design, whatever his reasoning and motivation. We know that Albert Pike made a Herculean effort to transform and improve the Scottish Rite, and there are many who rather cherish the idea he did just that.

Of all the many and numerous critics who registered their claims against, or simply critiquing, the authenticity of the Scottish Rite from the time of invention until the present day, one renowned and controversial occultist Arthur Waite (a gifted ritualist in his own right and co-designer of the Famous Rider-Waite Tarot Deck) was highly critical of his predecessor Albert Pike, and thought that his lack of knowledge and gift registered only failure, with regards to the Rite. Waite offers an extensive and elaborate assessment of General Pike's efforts in his 1937 revision of his own inspirational and informative work, The Secret Tradition in Freemasonry, and also his New Encyclopedia of Freemasonry. We will discuss Waite's vision and understanding with regards to Freemasonry, and the secret tradition therein, in pages to come, for now his views on Pike and Pike's influence on the Scottish Rite and greater world of Masonry remain our focus.

In The Secret Tradition in Freemasonry, Waite extensively criticizes the Scottish Rite, Pike's influence, and most especially Pike's magnum opus, Morals and Dogma; which according to Waite is merely a re-translation of French occultist Eliphas Levis' work, Transcendental Magic: Its Doctrine and Ritual (original translation by A. E. Waite), without credit or commentary! But this is not the limit of Pike's miscarriages and innovations; ultimately committing, in Waite's assessment, "...a permanent offense against logic. What amounts to such a drastic revision of the Scottish Rite began with amending the classification of the grades or degrees within the Rite; so much so, the Scottish Rite of North and South America no longer resembles the original sequence or substance of the old grades of the Council of Emperors of the East and West, a series of degrees and traditions wholly foreign and apart from the Craft Degrees system.[15]

The extent of the damage of Pike's influence went much further according to Waite, "...in the ritual transformations of the Ancient and Accepted Rite performed by A. Pike, a *new* spirit was brought into the subject matter of masonry and diverted it from its proper term..."[16] It is commonly known among Scottish Rite and Blue Lodge Masons that what Mackey "communicated" to Pike-in Pike's own words-amounted to a pile of rubbish almost completely useless aside from the Knight of the Rose Croix degree, of which it turns out there were some 20 different hand written versions of the ritual then in existence.

"So far as he (Pike) is concerned," Waite notes, "...there is no Royal Secret. He brought to his task of reconstruction, a commonplace mind stuffed with the waste matter of the Age of Reason...the Consistory is left with hands as empty as those with which we enter..."[17] Pike identified with French Masonry through the Continental Grades, and still more for adopting the revolutionary "device" in the form of the watchwords of the French Revolution, *"Liberty, Equality, Fraternity"*, which according to Waite is truly un-Masonic in origin which embraces "Faith, Hope, and Charity" as a motto. With this ideological declaration, Pike falsifies the great institution of Ancient Craft Masonry, which forever made the Scottish Rite a familiar example to be quoted, as illustrating Masonic teachings of an advanced anti-social and destructive character.[18]

Waite considered the Supreme Council of Charleston, South Carolina to be unscrupulous. Let us consider a moment the perspective from which Waite forms his opinions of Ancient Craft Masonry, Albert Pike and the Scottish Rite. "The Secret Tradition," Waite refers to in his book of this name, "...is like a–Holy Order that seeks to elevate the Craft out of a region of untinctured symbolism to the threshold of Divine Science."[19] With a distinct Eastern scope of understanding for a Westerner, Waite saw Brotherly Love in the Masonic Lodge as a reflection equal to the Sacred Unity of Hindu beliefs. It should also be noted that Waite recognized the importance of the Royal Arch (Capitular Degrees) and Cryptic Degrees as well for a complete understanding and application of the Ancient Craft Masonry educational system developed in the British Isles and modified in America.

For Waite, the system which progressively exposed the Candidate to a mystical pathway leading to the very porch of the Divine Temple within each one of us (which resonates with all aspects of the Craft Masonry system) fit together interlocking into a complete approach to ancient sources of Knowledge and Wisdom and Truth symbolically and emblematically encoded therein. To be very clear, the "ancient sources" referred to here are not necessarily or exclusively contained within the Craft Masonry System itself-it being simply one possible conduit with access to a far more ancient and pure expression of the Divine. The light of Divine Truth and Wisdom, referenced to and implied to be contained (or hidden) within each one of us, is dispensed refracted and reflected throughout the universe no matter what actions we take or do not take.

Each phase of development for the individual Mason is a step on the ascent to the pinnacle of understanding. The first three degrees of the

Blue Lodge are preparatory to exaltation to the Sublime Degree (or state) of the Holy Royal Arch. As Waite explains it, "...the Royal and Select Masters (Cryptic Degrees) throw light on the central point of the Royal Arch because they show us how a place of concealment was (and is) planned for the secret mysteries to be held..", in stasis outside the mainstream of consciousness, and how these mysteries remain "hidden" (or occulted) until time or circumstances (conditions) should render their revelation and restoration essential. [20] It seems Waite honestly believed that Pike was attempting, through his personal innovations and modifications to the Scottish Rite, to establish a new quasi-religious and paramilitary social order with the Supreme Council 33rd with his "chair" of Grand Commander as titular head of this.

Even more fascinating is his supposed method. According to Waite, Pike was employing a "base natural religion as blueprint" modified from the pseudo-transcendental magical system of Eliphas Levi. Waite's main contention stems from the perspective of a "Christian Knight"-a unique spiritual level of mystical development. He himself was a Knight of the Orders of Christian Mysteries, as well as a Rosicrucian Freemason, and he states, "...the Secret of Masonry that word too often lost, is the Secret of Christ realized in the heart of the Mason...".[21] Considering Pike a disciple of Levi, Waite simplifies Levi's esoteric philosophy as a negligible and ultimately failed construction based on the old sanctuaries of initiation, a magical or secret doctrine unworthy of our attention- "...participation in which was the end of all initiation."

From Waite's perspective, Pike was merely a clone of Levi, allocating the 32nd degree Prince of the Royal Secret as a presentation of Levi's secret magical doctrine. This doctrine, for both Levi and Pike, "...was only an elementary doctrine of 'equilibrium' the Kabbalistic mystery of balance..." with a distinct 8 fold path on which Waite further elaborates on page 620.[22] He concludes that Pike orchestrated an intervention of so-called Occult Philosophy under his own name while Levi, an archaic French occultist who was Jesuit-trained under the name Alphonse Constant, was the true author-of an ultimately meaningless teaching from the perspective of Craft Masonry. Nonetheless, Levi's teachings provided the backdrop to be overlaid upon the extant Scottish Rite Ritual and encoded with Pike's extraordinary and distinctly elaborated modifications.

We find in Waite's New Encyclopedia of Freemasonry "...as a critical scholar of Masonry, a historian, and a writer on the ethical and philosophical side of the subject he (Pike) is not to be taken as a guide, no man had a greater opportunity and no one a freer hand when he undertook to revise the Rituals of the Scottish Rite, and he scored only failure…"; The exception he takes with Pike's capacity and authority regarding Ancient Craft Masonry proper reiterating once more his charge that Pike foisted the brilliant, yet shallow, philosophia occulta of Eliphas Levi upon the unsuspecting reader as his own device through his revision of the Scottish Rite system, and Morals and Dogma, specifically. [23]

On page 440, Waite pronounces with finality, "…the Candidate for receiving the Sublime Prince of the Royal Secret degree is saluted as a Knight of St. Andrew and that of Prince Mason…the grade appears Templar in nature though destitute of symbolical importance or vital message of any kind." Aside from the Scottish Rite originating, according to Waite, from a fraudulent Latin charter under the name of Frederic the Great (very improbable, but no real virtue if true, considering the type of ruler Frederic was…) with no greater authority than any of the numerous other magnificent and spurious fabrications produced by various Masonic adventurers churning them out in the latter half of the 18th century. He concludes that "…it is abundantly evident that the Prince of the Royal Secret is neither itself alchemical nor a tolerable or rational introduction to a sequence of Hermetic Masonry", about which we are in fact very interested in learning, knowing and understanding. [24]

Maybe this is a good point at which to make clear that my main criticism of the Scottish Rite is not necessarily that the esoteric philosophies encoded therein are not valid and even useful learning systems for the student intent on that course of study per se. I am, however, suspicious of the innovative work of Pike and other agents in and around the Scottish Rite, Ancient Craft Masonry and the world at large and their rules of engagement; their modes operandi. I am concerned with the previously mentioned over-arching theme of a Secret War on Human Consciousness I believe is being prosecuted in all systems of learning and education-especially occult, esoteric and mystery traditions such as Freemasonry and other Western Lodge systems: the deliberate substitution of real knowledge and wisdom with counterfeit and over-simplified modifications and innovations, limited in scope and application. I am concerned with the designs of General Albert Pike and the National/International connections he enjoyed in his unique position in life public, private and secret.

In chapter eight of his postmodern treatise: The Secret Founding of America which is titled Freemasonry's Battle for America, author Nicholas Hagger tells us the Scottish Rite, working closely with foreign bankers connected with European "Illuminati orders", had been taking control of America's Federal Government soon after its formation in 1787. In 1851, Giuseppe Mazzini-who controlled the Italian incarnation of supposed Illuminati though obviously not the original group-formed revolutionary groups throughout the United States to intensify debate on slavery and hopefully spark a civil war. "Young American" Lodges modeled after "Young Italy" Lodges were organized. All controlled by Mazzini agents using Cincinnati Lodge #133 as their headquarters.[25] There are many letters between Pike and Mazzini indicating shared interests and goals. Pike was also active in Young American Lodges.

Hagger tells us Franklin Peirce made a deal with Mazzini, for support of the Young Americans, to get into the White House-which amounted to Cabinet appointments for Scottish Rite/quasi-Illuminati operatives within the Presidential Administration. During this time, in 1853, Albert Pike was communicated the degrees of the Scottish Rite by Albert Mackey and returned home to Arkansas with the loose leaf rituals of the Rite to commence editing the work. Four years later, Pike traveled to New Orleans eventually receiving the 33rd degree and in 1859 was appointed/elected Sovereign Grand Commander of the Southern Jurisdiction of the Ancient and Accepted Scottish Rite in Charleston. Not long after this the Civil War broke out, beginning with the famous battle at Fort Sumter on April 12th 1861-which was, by the way, within ear and eye shot of the Supreme Council 33rd Degree headquarters in Charleston.

U.S. Attorney General Caleb Cushing (appointed by Peirce) had ties to the Scottish Rite Northern Jurisdiction and Albert Pike through their mutual affiliation with a little known chivalric order from the South called the Order of the Knights of the Golden Circle (according to Hagger, as well as Bob Brewer, author of In the Shadow of the Sentinel, and many other internet researchers). The name "Golden Circle" referred to a proposed slave empire that would encompass all the southern states of the U.S., much of Mexico, Central America, and the northern part of South America. With Havana as its center, this so-called "slavocracy" would produce the world's supply of cotton, sugar, tobacco, etc.

According to Hagger, the Knights of the Golden Circle formed as an order in 1858 steeped in the novels of Walter Scot (Ivanhoe, Rob Roy), and immediately absorbed many Freemasons. Working with the Young

Americans, Albert Pike opened a "Castle" (chapter) of the Knights of the Golden Circle in New Orleans. Many more Castles opened, spreading through the South and Southwest of America. These Pseudo-Arthurian Knights, riding around the countryside supposedly doing good deeds for 'Dixie', created a fertile fantasy ideal which the romantic southern mind proved receptive to and many men were recruited into the ranks.

Meanwhile, the many moves on the checkerboard pavement of the Government positions and Operatives, and their affiliates, are almost impossible to track without some confusion-nonetheless we will attempt to retrace and recount the machinations leading up to the Civil War. Caleb Cushing, mentioned above, seems one of many key players in the events which led to the Civil War. Appointed Attorney General to the Peirce Administration in 1853, he is speculated to be a factor in bringing the North and South into collision over slavery by encouraging the Peirce Admin to pass the Kansas/Nebraska Act of 1854, which allowed the inhabitants of the newly formed states of Kansas and Nebraska to decide whether or not to allow slavery. John Brown was supposedly a member of Mazzini's Young Americans Lodge and a former Master Mason with ties to Cushing, through the John Jacob Astor Senior interests in Boston and New York.

In 1857, Buchanan (another Freemasonic President) was elected and John Quitman, founder of the Knights of the Golden Circle in Jackson, Mississippi, was nominated as the new Sovereign Grand Commander of the Supreme Council Southern Jurisdiction; but he dies suddenly (it is speculated possibly from poison) and Albert Pike is nominated instead, by Cushing a key player in Southern succession, and is elected to become the leader of the Scottish Rite.

Most of the Confederate Military leadership, according to Hagger, was composed of Scottish Rite Freemasons and the Knights of the Golden Circle all secretly under the sway of Albert Pike and the Supreme Council 33rd. Once again, as with Peirce, under Buchanan many key cabinet positions are occupied by Scottish Rite operatives. Attorney General Howell Cobb, of Georgia, was made a 33rd degree March 1860 and helped organize the Confederacy in Montgomery, Alabama. President Buchanan appointed John Floyd as Secretary of War, who then proceeded to sell 10,000 rifles from the U.S. Government to the State of South Carolina, which effectively served to arm the secessionists before he was made Brigadier General of the Confederate Army. Buchanan's Vice President was John Breckinridge of Kentucky.

31

During the 1860 Democratic National Convention in Charleston-the headquarters for the Supreme Council Southern Jurisdiction-Cushing, who was President of the convention, was made Chair to the secessionists Convention and elected Breckinridge as their Candidate for President. Breckinridge also received the 33rd degree from Pike in March 1860. On December 20, 1860, South Carolina, the headquarters of the Southern Jurisdiction of the Scottish Rite, was the first State to secede after Lincoln was elected President. The Secretary of War then sent 124 cannons to unfinished forts along the southern border-where they could be seized by insurrectionists-continuing to indirectly arm the South for the war to come. Many southern States followed South Carolina in seceding from the Union, all led by men who already were or would soon become 33rd Degree Inspector Generals. One thousand armed Knights of the Golden Circle forced Sam Houston, then Texas Governor, to secede in February, 1861. The Knights were later foiled in their first attempt to assassinate Lincoln in March 1861, by General Winfield Scott.

In April 1861, Knight of the Golden Circle General Beauregard was ordered to surprise attack Fort Sumter, which began the Civil War officially. Lincoln was not a Freemason and he fought against foreign banking interests in America-needless to say-this created many enemies along with those from the slavery issue and the Civil War. Many groups called for Lincoln to be overthrown and worse. John Wilkes Booth was both a 33rd Scottish Rite Freemason and a Knight of the Golden Circle and supposedly a member of the Young Americans Lodge (new evidence comes to light suggesting he may also have been an operative for an early government secret service-his acting career a perfect front)!

According to Bob Brewer (author of In the Shadow of the Sentinel), legendary bank robber Jesse James, also a 33rd Degree and a member of the Knights of the Golden Circle, was assigned to rob Northern banks to fund a new Civil War. It is believed he may have hidden up to $7 Billion in various caches which were never recovered officially, or at least not reported. The exposure of the Knights of the Golden Circle, in the Assassination trials of 1865, was so emphatic that the Knights disbanded officially in 1867, by many accounts folding into the Order of the Ku Klux Klan, the name taken from the Greek, "kuklos", for circle.[26] Pike referred to it as an "Order of Southern Brotherhood."

As we have already mentioned, General Pike was in fact arrested in connection with the murder of President Lincoln due to his multiple affiliations with many Knights and conspirators; which speaks for itself as to the condition of his character in the eyes of law and order. Pike was tried and found guilty of treason, for his involvement and conduct in the Civil War; as Brigadier General in command during the infamous Battle of Pea Ridge, Arkansas-Pike's troops were accused of immoral conduct on the battlefield not only mutilating corpses but also collecting scalps and other morbid trophies.

But Benjamin French, 33rd degree member of the Board of Directors of the Supreme Council along with other men of influence, pressured President Johnson to pardon Pike in 1865. Several months later, Johnson received a delegation of SR officials in his bedroom at the White House and was communicated, by Albert Pike himself, the 4th-32nd degrees of the Scottish Rite "…as an honorarium."

It is here that I would posit the "Military Industrial Educational Complex" of America was midwifed into existence and we will explore this further–in the next chapter. At this point we begin to see how the Scottish Rite made inroads into all the most influential positions within American Society, under the auspices of a noble cause and laudable pursuit and all the while Stewarded by the mysterious character Albert Pike, whose eleven foot statue in Washington, D.C. dubs him "the Merlin of Masonry."

4

THE SECRET WAR

ON HUMAN CONSCIOUSNESS

At this point we need to shift gears and expand our focus, widen the lens, in order to peer at the big picture for a moment-the overarching theme I keep alluding to, the title of this chapter, the main thrust of my argument, the how and whys needed to fill in the blank spots.

A secret war is being waged on human consciousness in the guise of the 21st century never-ending need for security, which manifests most apparently in ever-expanding militarization. It is a war of the global corporate elite against all other life on Earth, and against the awakening of consciousness in the masses. The origins of this war on consciousness in the United States are obvious in its military history. Fear is the pathogen. Thus every generation is imprinted with a false flag "fear" event inoculant to reinforce the fear paradigm and upgrade the meme. The great shift from the "founding" of the U.S. and its "colonial" phase to the full-on establishment of the military-industrial-educational global super power commenced with the American Indian and Civil Wars of the 19th century.

The U.S. Civil War (1861-1864) furthered the industrialization, militarization and social engineering of the new nation. Most of the major decisive battles of the Civil War were within 20 miles of a railroad stop. The South was at a disadvantage since its riverboats were excellent for transporting cotton and tobacco but not so good at transporting the weight of horses, cannons, and soldiers. Northern control of the railroad gave them a decided advantage. Thus when the War Between the States finally ceased, the railroad barons dominated the new born industrialized military.

A powerful hybrid is the union of corporate fascism: the combination of corporate power and military might. Their power was so great that when the Democratic candidate Samuel Tilden of Rochester, NY won both the popular and electoral votes in the 1876 election, he *still* was not allowed to become President, thanks to some 20 odd electoral votes contested. Instead, Civil War General Rutherford B. Hayes, the Republican candidate, was "awarded" the presidency in the Compromise of 1877: the Democrats gave the White House to Hayes and his railroad baron backers in exchange for the Republican release of the South, their

Civil War hostage, withdrawing federal troops and ending the Reconstruction (social engineering program) in the South.

In the interest of expanding the coal, oil and railroad baron's empires, newly "awarded" President Hayes declared war on the remaining native peoples in the West and their unique tribal cultures. Domestic genocide plus the quasi-Prussian schooling system and compulsory education legislation began the consolidation of a "hive" national consciousness. Literacy standards and critical thinking were degraded as a collective consciousness rooted in obedience and nationalistic consumerism was set in place. The American psyche has never been the same, individually or collectively. From the Modern to Post-modern to Electronic age, persuasive civic mythologies and faith-based belief systems have followed.

From the 1898 Spanish-American War false-flag media cry "Remember the Maine!", for the sinking of the Maine and hundreds of U.S. sailors in Havana Harbor; to the "Great War" precipitator-the sinking of the Lusitania-loaded to the gills with explosives, weapons and civilians and sent directly into German U-boat infested waters; to the Pearl Harbor sacrifice of 2,000 sailors for the cause of the "European Civil War", as WWII was referred to before that fateful day in December 1941; to the Gulf of Tonkin incident in 1964 which sparked the Vietnam "conflict"; to the "Terrorist attack " of September 11th, 2001; all of these reported attacks, and many more, were and are all war propaganda sculpted and fabricated to illicit a desired response from the general public.

Is this really the best we can come up with? Can we not imagine another vision of reality than war and violence against each other, so as to break free of the conditioning we have been subjected to since the very beginning of this nation-state of nation-states in general?

Misdirection alone works to effectively distract the American psyche from the true state of reality so it will adhere to a classic romantic-existential angst of supposed and perceived separation, and disconnection, from the vast active living intelligence system that surrounds and connects us all to higher states of consciousness and divine awareness.

What I propose is the creation of a new civic mythology for our present Post-Modern-Electronic State, a true mystical Grail Quest: to recover the lost Sacred Feminine, the Creative Mind of the Universe, the in-dwelling Spirit of Divine Wisdom known to the ancients as Gaia Sophia, Earth Wisdom Goddess, perceived by the "Gnostics" as the creator of all life on Earth. The Gaia Principle once restored the Sacred

Feminine brought back into balance and union with the Divine Masculine principle within all consciousness in accordance with the universal law of gender. Some cite the Gaia Hypothesis as yet another elite-sanctioned and subsidized subterfuge, or intelligence agency COINTELPRO operation, and of course it is difficult to be absolutely certain of anything. Many years ago I realized that humanity had been captivated, thoroughly indoctrinated and imprinted, with the teachings and outlooks of the "Abrahamic" religious meme.

I realized that on the most fundamental level, an elaborate thought-stopping mechanism was embedded within the main religions of the world all classic victim/perpetrator mind control programs, effectively weakening any resistance to the exclusive inhumane mindset of a strictly hostile patriarchy and its one-sided approach to reality and all life on Earth. It was perfectly self-perpetuating by design, and the result?

Our species suffers from acute "de-sacralization": the devaluation and removal of the Sacred from our everyday collective and individual awareness as well as more sublime states of consciousness. Discord thus locks us into routine patterns of mediocrity and outright captivity. As Manly P. Hall described it: "We have lost sublimity of the everyday and as a result we cannot satisfy our imaginations nor can we nourish the idealism of our constitutions…"

Thus formed The Wasteland…

"What then is the wasteland? It is the land where myth is patterned by authority, not emergent from life; where there is no poet's eye to see, no adventure to be lived, where all is set for all and forever….utopia!"
-Joseph Campbell, Creative Mythology (1959)

What then is the remedy for this condition? What would cure what ails humanity? One "treatment" is a direct and active response, a form of "bio-mysticism", an empathic and visionary participation in the life-force. [27] Our only hope is that by contemplating the animation of the material and sensory world, we might move into deeper rapport with the mysterious indwelling spirit which is the source of all life itself.

Gnosis is a method of direct access to the physics of the cosmos through the finely tuned instrument of the human body, an energetic transceiver through the senses or "bio-physics of perception", according to Austrian genius Wilhelm Reich. By infusing imagination with sacred elements and direct contact with the life force of Nature, we can restore mythical and mystical patterns of human awareness and experience to our reality.

Synchronicity is connected to the transmission of Gnosis through cosmic consciousness, especially where synchronicity is defined as "...the discovery of convergent archetypal symbols in media and pop culture acting as the very undercurrent of divine awareness personified through the myriad processes and symbols that make up the building blocks of conscious reality." [28] The natural law of correspondence comes into play here as above so below as within so without. The greater reality is reflected, contained within the lesser.

We are clearly living in the aftermath of a species-wide hijacking of human consciousness. Numerous sources conclude that some 10-13,000 years ago, one or more earth-shattering catastrophes effectively knocked humanity's collective network of consciousness, as well as individual consciousness, offline. This created, in effect, a species-wide post-traumatic stress disorder (PTSD) if you will. In such a weakened state, the human species was ripe for exploitation. Enter a pathogen, a "mind virus" infestation of indeterminate source, an inner/outer species predator that "grokked" the terra incognita of the human mindscape. This collective disorder diverted enough of humanity from a tribal hunter-gatherer subsistence lifestyle to a city-state agricultural system with authority justified and reinforced by a select priesthood, chosen for obedience and skill, perpetuating the ruling paradigm. The collective species paradigm was brought back online, gradually under a veritable "safe mode"; a fire-walled version of reality not unlike the Chinese model of the Internet, a deliberately narrowed bandwidth of frequency that can easily be manipulated.

Down through the ages there has always been a struggle, a constant battle between the darkness and the light. In one form or another two schools of esoteric knowledge employing Mystery Traditions governed by Universal Laws of Consciousness always arise. For the sake of this discussion, we will call one path, the "Illuminators", those who commenced to instruct and liberate those initiated and the other the "Illuminati", those who entrapped and enslaved the followers of this path. The Illuminators were "phosters" (as in phosphorescent), light guides to divine wisdom; their tools and approaches guided initiates to full integration, realization, and actualization. The Illuminati, on the other hand, employed many of the same techniques, traditions and laws of consciousness to bind their adherents to a false reality; dead-end rabbit

37

holes of simulated inorganic chaos.

Communication plays a pivotal role in constructing and maintaining how we experience the world around us, a world defined by a particular map of reality, a particular way of looking at the universe. Human-to-human experience thus has a potent influence on the way people understand themselves and their world, however constructed. Secret schools and religious orders are formed to preserve and transmit powerful universal knowledge as the ebb and flow of human consciousness shifts. Secret orders **should** protect knowledge from being misused and exploited, but they just as often keep knowledge from the masses to be used by the elite to maintain their control. Today's un-restrained science and technologies are evidence of how knowledge, without ethics and integration of consciousness, has been and still is a menace to the world.

As we have touched upon in preceding chapters, English Craft Masonry is a modified hybrid of the Stone Mason's Lodges systems left over from the traditions of the Roman Comicine Guilds, woven in with various alchemical, hermetic and occult systems and traditions, all forced underground by ecclesiastical authority and persecution. The Mystery teachings encoded into Lodge systems initially represented a form of Protestant mysticism for Renaissance man and those of the Enlightenment-an alternative to the Jesuit/Papal control of, and intrusion into, individual interactions with the Divine. Thus secrecy began as a way of surviving persecution and the Vatican Inquisition; "heresy" deriving from the Greek, "Hairesis", meaning "to choose" an alternative path or outlook on creation and the universe. Needless to say, the Catholic, or "universal", church had zero tolerance for Hermetic magical occulted systems.

The cloak-and-dagger apparatus of esoteric orders-passwords, signs of recognition, etc...-employed secrecy as a security device, to weed out potential threats or freeloading imposters; as many lodges offered financial and social benefits well worth having. In colonial America, where lodges eventually opened their doors to a wider class of society, such benefits helped to sustain a colonial brother mason and even whole communities in times of need. Today, we live in the midst of an extraordinarily complex worldwide web of communication that reinforces specific ways of thinking about everything. The stronger and more consistent the messages of this Web, the more difficult it is to step outside of a particular map of the world to understand that the world can be seen in a completely different way. This "Web effect" creates a deadening uniformity of thought.

Finding ways to break out of this Web effect is an obvious approach to overcoming lock-step uniformity and consensus. Nearly all spiritual systems provide a variety of methods for doing this, the simplest and most common method being the solitary monastic path.

Another path lies in esoteric secrets that, by their very nature, create a *gap* in awareness; placing the specific item of information outside of that everyday Web of communication, so that some information does not become part of the map of the world shared by the rest of society. If the secret is something painful or destructive, or imposed by force rather than freely chosen, the breach in the Web can lead to madness; but if secrecy is freely chosen, and kept, it becomes a tool with remarkable powers and a wide range of constructive and healthy uses for reshaping awareness.

A secret forms a link between its keeper and the realities not included in the Web of everyday life. A bridge forms, a space between worlds that can heighten and reshape consciousness on a quantum level that is more open and better prepared to perceive symbolic, emblematic and allegorical communications and transmissions far beyond every day perceptual experience. Secrecy thus serves as a potent method of empowering the self-discipline that transforms an individual's psychic relationship with the experiential world. This inner and more esoteric aspect of secrecy is what makes it so useful as a *delivery system* imperceptibly synchronized with consciousness, like how Tarot images-especially the 22 trumps of the Major Arcana-transmit the ancient wisdom and tradition encoded in each card. It turns out that a picture really is worth a thousand words. This is the level we reach through ritual preparation to receive such knowledge.

Our world is under a spell, a vast global enchantment, in the iron grip of sensory materialism-conditioned experience, so-called "scientific" observation and investigation to the exclusion of all else. The ancient idea that the physical universe is only *part* of creation has been all but lost. The non-physical, or metaphysical (from the Greek for *beyond* the physical), was and is just as real, though beyond the meager frequency range of our five senses. We must retrain our minds in order to view the greater reality and see through the false realities being shaped by cybernetic social engineering and mind control programs, trans-humanist dystopias and multi-media virtual realities managed by a break-away predatory society, foisting upon us the false paradigm of closed energy systems and artificial scarcity and shortages. The largest multi-generational mind control operation ever perpetrated upon humanity a four-pronged assault by media, arts and sciences, industry, and military/government/intelligence agencies must be thrown off.

Western esoteric systems, occult sciences, Mystery teachings and traditions are tools and devices for inviting transformative change in consciousness. These vehicles can transport us into altered and heightened states, so that we can "step into the circuitry of the cosmos", as Master Initiate Lon Milo Duquette words it, and come into conscious contact with divine intelligence(s).

The Lodge itself is one of these vehicles. Not unlike the T.A.R.D.I.S. the blue police box of the Dr. Who television series, the lodge defies time and space. The ritual of the Blue Lodge gives the construction, layout, dimensions of the lodge structure as an oblong square facing east to west-which seems normal enough. Within the Lodge structure we are told the dimension span from the canopy of heaven (the ceiling of the lodge being the blue canopy of heaven above hence the name "Blue" Lodge) to the center of the earth and to the east and the west as far as the eye can see. Clearly the Lodge like the T.A.R.D.I.S. defies the normal laws of physics by this description. And like Dr. Who's vehicle we move between worlds within the Lodge. Like the brain itself the contents within are limitless.

The outrageous statement made by mainstream science and medicine that 90% of our DNA is "junk", a view now thrown out, seeks to shut down our grey-matter much like the Chinese Internet firewalled against individual choice.

Methods of awakening, or reawakening/reactivating, consciousness beyond the everyday Web have always existed. The ancient world's hermetic axiom, *As above, so below*, implied that all aspects of reality-from physical to metaphysical-manifest in orderly sequences, just as Hermes the Thrice Great declared. All things follow an immense pattern, a greater reality, a sum totality simultaneously contained like a Mandelbrot within each lesser part. Solving the mystery of a lesser reality, such as one's small life, is indeed the key to the mystery of the Greater Reality in an infinite feedback loop threading through micro- and macro-consciousness.

The dilemma of everyday awareness remains, with most people locked in the frequency bandwidth of sensory materialism. The once knowable and accessible elements of higher consciousness have devolved, categorized and filtered into a blind cul-de-sac of the unknowable with slavish deference to "experts," and those who are capable of any sort of critical thinking often throw themselves into material science. In this rationalist's nightmare, humanity's worth is measured by the hour and dollar, and the invisible causes of life are downgraded to myth, legend and fantasy; not to be believed in.

But all hope is not lost! Consider the principles of "sync"; synchronicity and synchro-mysticism, deriving meaningful patterns from seemingly unrelated events and from the universe at large. Etheric ambient signal transmissions and combinations of high frequency broadband, radio, television and analog signals are all there in a supreme cosmic feedback loop. The universe is speaking to our brains through the language of Sync. A 21st century techno-mysticism is passing down transcendental wisdom through seemingly random messages, contrasted with a deep affinity for the ambient life-force from which we can learn and grow despite the social engineering and mind control programs. *Our own recognition and belief play a huge part in shaping reality.*

Consciousness and reality are interwoven in an intimate interaction with an energetic and holographic multiverse. Our physical bodies are individual wet-cell quantum processors downloading customized operating systems from the Supreme Divine Administrator of the cosmic network we call our reality. Within this quantum entanglement, the Divine Admin fabricates material existence upon a canvas of photonic plasma and dark space/matter, or so the great minds of science tell us.

Max Igan, from thecrowhouse.com, suggests that conscious intelligence-cosmic or otherwise-transmits "hydraulically" thru the medium of water; hydrogen being the original atom or particle of matter in existence. He posits that when one's bodily vehicle finally degrades and shuts down, its 60% water content is expelled and re-collected by the Gaian (Earth) Matrix, effectively uploading the sum of our individual life experiences back to the source of consciousness. In effect, a network upgrade occurs with every passing. Hence the focus on global control and alchemical manipulation of world water supplies and sources.

The seven ancient principles of Natural Law or the Universal Laws of Consciousness: mentalism, correspondence, vibration, polarity, rhythm, cause and effect, and gender, are at the root of every Mystery tradition and esoteric system. They are not merely good guides to awareness but are phenomenological facts, as inevitable and unavoidable as gravity and thermo-dynamics are in our 3D reality.

For myself, I realized I must *re*-learn these truths because they had been so effectively hijacked and deactivated within my own psyche. For too long have I and my people participated in the genocidal enslavement of our own species indentured by ignorance, fear and coercion.

The greatest coercive method is education, or more to the point, compulsion schooling. To say that school was a negative experience for me would be an understatement; a short conversation with my parents will uncover reports of one episode or issue after another, all through my primary and secondary education. At age 16, during my second run through the tenth grade, also my second time being kept back due to incompletions, I decided to withdraw from high school. Nine years later I completed my general equivalency test received a diploma and enrolled in University. I actually did very well in secondary schooling holding a solid 3.4 GPA, or a B+ average. I was also elected president of the Philosophy Club in my freshman year, which was unprecedented at UMass. I only chose to leave University because of the economic stranglehold the Government and the banks put unto the working class student in order to attend. I realized I could just as easily, more productively and cost effectively, pursue a course of independent study.

It wasn't until years after I left high school that I realized what had happened. I picked up a book off of the old Border's bookstore shelf and sat down in an overstuffed chair for a good read. The book was called The Underground History of American Education by John Taylor Gatto, a teacher and 30+ year veteran of the New York Public and private school systems, and winner of the prestigious teacher of the year award in New York City. He responded to this honor by resigning from teaching and by touring America, with the indictment that we were being uniformly dumbed-down as a nation and society!

I read Gatto's break down, description and details of the elaborate and multi-faceted, multi-generational program of institutionalized social engineering of the United States populace. And I wept tears of complete and utter validation for what I had personally experienced. For what Mr. Gatto explained to me, was the history of how the education system in America had evolved. And a picture began to form in my mind of a timeline which would become my theory of the secret war on human consciousness years later. Suddenly, I understood why I felt such adversity to the entire system of public and private education. In fact, my parents had worked hard to eventually send me to private schools, seeking a higher level of learning for me; though ultimately, all was for naught as I could not move past the inherently inhumane treatment schooling seemed to me.

Having been raised in an artistic household, books, music, and art supplies were made readily available to me. As a boy I was read to regularly and drew pictures with my mother often, especially hidden pictures where we would both drew a scene with several elements hidden within the picture that the observer had to locate. I was allowed to question everything that was proposed to or expected of me. I was also extremely defiant to all forms of authority over me.

I learned from Mr. Gatto that the core curriculum of public schools in America is training us in three fundamental principles, or tenets, of conduct:

1. Show up on time! Don't be late it was imprinted in us as a moral issue complete with public humiliation as reinforcement.

2. Obey your keeper/instructor/supervisor. Do what you are told without question and do it quickly.

3. Do the mindless, seemingly meaningless task before you, for the slotted amount of time, and when the bell rings clean up and exit the work space until your next scheduled shift.

It is conformity and behaviorism at its highest level, and as Mr. Gatto further illustrates in his work, this training produces good little soldiers, industrial workers, and consumers. To put it quite simply, the sum total of public school education is a multi-layered elaborate system of obedience training. He maps out the structures of real growth in learning "...growth and mastery come only to those who vigorously self-direct. Initiating, creating, doing, reflecting, freely associating, enjoying privacy- these are precisely what the structures of schooling are set up to prevent, on one pretext or another". [29] Dense urban populations, especially in ghetto minority areas and the rural South, were the first targeted regions for compulsion schooling in America.

It was through a series of "traveler's reports" that were published in the early 1800's that information about the Prussian system of education was brought to the attentions of the architects of the American education system. One very influential report came from French philosopher Victor Cousin, where he praised Prussia for finding new ways to "contain the danger of a frightening new social phenomenon, the industrial proletariat" which was so convincing that after being instituted in France, it was found that "French children could be stupefied as easily as German ones." Meanwhile, here at home, the labor oriented new state of Michigan was "mimicking Prussian organization... established the first State Superintendency of education in 1833. With a state minister and state control entering all aspects of schooling, the only missing ingredient was compulsion legislation". [30]

This happened under the direction of one William Pierce, a Unitarian Minister from Rochester, New York. Due to his known associations with French and German "Scotch Masons", he had been accused of concealing a 'Lodge of the Illuminati" behind the façade of his church, and fled across the Great Lakes to Michigan to escape personal harm during Anti-Masonic furor just before the first Jackson election, and there his connections proved capable of securing him this very important administrative position in America's newly forming education systems and production centers. Calvin Stowe (husband of Harriet Beecher) reported to the Ohio State Legislature "attesting to Prussian superiority... widely distributed across the country, the Ohio group mailing out 10,000 copies and the legislatures of Massachusetts, Michigan, Pennsylvania, North Carolina, and Virginia each reprinting and distributing the document." [31]

What was so special about the Prussian model? After Napoleon's lightning campaign defeat of Prussian in 1806, the Prussian military industrial leadership determined the root cause of their defeat was too strong of social ties to family and village in the soldiers; too great a will to live and survive the battle and return home to the hearth. The average infantry man on the frontline would rather live to fight another day than lay his life down for the State. Soon after this, in 1812, America suffered an equally demoralizing defeat against the British who sacked Washington D.C. and burned the White House and Capitol building. The President fled on horseback like a thief in the night running for his life. The "war-like nation" that was Prussia had a great deal of material and military prosperity throughout the 19th century.

"While German science, philosophy, and military success seduced the whole world, thousands of prominent young Americans made the pilgrimage to Germany to study in its network of research universities places where teaching and learning were always subordinate to investigations done on behalf of business and the State. Returning home with the coveted German PhD, those so degreed became University

Presidents and department heads, took over private industrial research bureaus, government offices and the administrative professions. The men they...hired...were those who found it morally agreeable to offer obeisance to the Prussian outlook...in this leveraged fashion the gradual takeover of American Mental life managed itself."[32]

It was determined that the new military/industrial revolution required a new soldier, and worker, to turn its wheels and use its weapons: a man with nothing preventing him from self-sacrifice, nothing to make him pause or even hesitate to lay his life down for the State if that is what he or she is called to do. Prussia spear-headed the campaign to reform education to meet the State needs. The course of action, as Gatto describes, was simple; the state must break up the family hearth that was the power center of culture and society. Remove the children from the household through compulsion schooling laws and child labor restrictions, effectively shutting down apprenticeship, then send first father and next mother off to work in the mine and factory. The child, economically orphaned as a member of the labor class, is raised with an exploitable psycho-social hampering which effectively hobbles his conscience and increases his or her susceptibility to manipulation and coercion, as well as a readiness to commit inhumane acts.

The other major testimonial to Prussian schooling came in the form of Horace Mann's Seventh Report to the Boston School Committee (1843) which ranked Prussia number one of all nations in schooling, England coming in last. The resolutely non-intellectual subject matter of Prussian Volksschulen was praised; "grouping by age, multiple layers of supervision, and selective training for teachers... Wrote Mann, 'There are many things there which we should do well to imitate.'"; though he had not actually seen a school in session as he had visited Prussia during the summer when the schools were closed. [33]

Shortly thereafter, the Association of Masters of the Boston Public Schools issued a rebuttal to Mann's report, criticizing the schooling proposals as "a vehicle of propaganda for Mann's 'hot bed theories' in which the projectors have disregarded experience and observation." They also attacked the "teacher-centered, non-book presentations" of the Prussian system, making the claim that the goal in this was to "break student potential for forming habits of independent individual effort."[34]

Before the advent of state-reformed compulsion education, learning in school was literature driven; revolving around the study of literature and research journals. Gatto informs us that literacy before, and right after, the Revolution in America was in the range of 100 percent of the colonial population, and that literacy among the slave populations was near 75 %(!); reminding us, after all, that literacy drove the revolution, with the pamphleteers sculpting public opinion through their written words. Today's standard of literacy is in the range of 40 percent, and this is defined as "functional literacy" in that one can read and follow printed instructions; as in operating manuals and the like rather than reading to comprehend and expound rhetorically and logically on a given subject matter.

Many of JP Morgan's interests were instrumental in bringing Prussian schooling to the prostrate South after the Civil War. Andrew Carnegie's "Gospel of Wealth", which became extremely popular at the advent of the transformation of American education, the idea that the wealthy "owed society a duty to take over everything in the public interest... The defining characteristic of class control is that it establishes a grammar and vocabulary for ordinary people, and for subordinate elites, too." [35] Carnegie was a steel magnate, and one Mr. Gatto credits with feeding into the notion of "cradle-to-grave schooling", instituting a disconnect between families from a very young age, as well as promoting the authority of the educators.

During the span of one lifetime, the utopic ideal of an orderly collective society that had been channeled, via small elite groups, throughout history in an almost continuous fashion since the time of classical Egypt, was brought to fruition, and the U.S. was transformed from a place "where human variety had ample room to display itself to a laboratory of virtual orthodoxy-a process concealed by dogged survival of the mythology of independence..." With New England as the testing ground for this initiative, and now primed and ready to take advantage of the period of mass-immigration and "opportunity of mass regimentation afforded by the Civil War to establish this form of total State... The plan advanced in barely perceptible stages, each new increment making it more difficult for individual families to follow an independent plan...It was the end of Thomas Jefferson's dream, the final betrayal of democratic promise in the last new world on the planet." [36]

It was important to displace the true homegrown Western systems of liberation and actualization achieved through myth, legend, language, art and culture in order to enforce the industrialization of society; corporate socialism and corporate capitalism converge to produce a truly organized society with the State behind the proverbial wheel, "run by a

46

managerial class and professional politicians, both thoroughly materialistic in outlook; both (organizing) human masses into a centralized system... In both, alienated corporate man—well-fed, well-clothed, well-entertained—is governed by bureaucrats. At the end of history men are not slaves but robots...the vision of utopia seen complete." [37] And it has been refitted to reflect the model of compulsion schooling in order to produce an obedient and productive society from childhood onto elder age.

The process was commenced through children's literature, and later through "education". A feeling of indifference to family was fostered as children were invited, through suggestion, to divide their interests from the interests of their families. The Post Civil War period saw an increase of children's books with characters looking within to their own needs and desires; previously most stories dealt with issues of a redemptive nature or where "strength, afforded by stable community life, was an important part of narrative action... toward the end of the nineteenth century a totally new note of 'self' was sounded. Now protagonists became more competent, more in control; their need for family and communal affirmation disappeared, to be replaced by a new imperative...the individual child *free from the web of family and community*." [38] The concept of child labor became a negative, and delaying entry into the workforce until teenage or later was encouraged, even though apprenticeship was the quickest and most reliable way for anyone to gain independence; the obvious method of success used by all the industrialists who were now intent on shutting down the practice.

To what end would these social scientists and industrialists be working towards with their careful crafting of our society? On September 13, 1909, some 60 years after Mann's *Seventh Report*, George Reynolds, the president of the American Bankers Association, stood before a gathering of his peers singing the praises of "a 'Federal Reserve' of centralized, private banking interests; modeled after the German Reichsbank"; a masterfully coordinated move by the industrialists and financiers in an attempt to transfer control over money and interest rates from elected representatives to a central banking system. [39] Then on September 14, 1909 in Boston, President Taft, advised the nation that it should "take up seriously the problem of establishing a centralized bank on the German model." [40] I think it is pretty clear how that worked out for the American people.

5

THE USURPATION OF FREEMASONRY

As I have stated already in this work, I have taken a more romantic quixotic approach to life. As a young man I strayed from the warm campfires of human civilization into the outer regions of the streets, highways, byways, forests, deserts and mountains of America; most times on foot with only a backpack full of worldly possessions; drifting on the road and having many interesting experiences and adventures that will fill the pages of another book. It would suffice to say I have travelled many roads to get here. With romantic notions, I searched for America's lost zeitgeist-the spirit of our times. What I found wandering the streets in the towns and cities of America, more often than not, was a postmodern wasteland of under-employment, pollution and despair…and pockets of affluence, along with what might be called a sub- or counter-culture; what Jack Kerouac called the "fellaheen" society's forgotten rejects, reprobates and recidivists living off the leftover scraps on the outskirts of civilization. It was quite disillusioning at times, though often inspiring, and always educational.

Having taken an extended hiatus from school to tramp across America, I returned from the road and reenrolled in University in pursuit of a degree in Philosophy. I quickly realized the sham that is so-called "higher learning" in America and its predatory lending practices in league with the banks. After two years I withdrew, opting to continue independent study for free.

Moving past that time in my life, I met my best friend in the whole world; my loving and supportive wife, partner and co-conspirator in life. When I started the radio show, she took on the moniker of "Mater X" to keep the continuity with my assumed identity and ran the show chat-room, developing a rapport with our listeners. While we raised our four amazing children I continued to study and research numerous interrelated subjects and topics, including the extensive research I did tracing my family history back to Scotland in the mid 1600's through to 9th century Ireland. A pattern and picture of a different reality than what I had known began to form.

I realized in the wake of my research that the European Tribes of ancient times had been stripped of their true culture just as the Tribal

Indians of America had-simply one thousand years earlier. I also realized the Mystery Schools and Esoteric Traditions were systems which contained the vital remains of Western Spirituality before the corruption of the Abrahamic Religious infestation. This, more than anything, led me to the doors of the Temple; the ancient meaning of which is "place of learning and instruction". I joined the Lodge to know the truth; to infiltrate the lion's den, and possibly recapture the lost mysteries of my own people. I came to see the so-called "Mysteries" as humanity's lost spiritual legacy.

I had the benefit of being raised by an extraordinary woman; my mother is an artist, writer, painter, sculptor and Master Gardener. Her creative approach to reality was imprinted on me at a very early age. She also dabbled in real magick in the 80's and 90's, joining women studies groups and new age energy groups; all of which helped her to process her own life experiences, and led her to becoming, in her own right, a practitioner of a modified form of Wicca. As a matter of fact, my mother was the first one who presented to me the systems of ceremonial magic and occult studies as viable tools for self-help, self-actualization integration and revelation.

And so my path was set: doing extensive research into all things occulted and esoteric, I was armed with knowledge many Freemason's within the Lodge had not acquired. I therefore rose with relative ease inside the Lodge system. I was tapped to join some very prestigious side orders on the merit of my knowledge and understanding. I was also given access to libraries and collections of material which shed greater light on the origins and true reality of the Esoteric Fraternal Orders, particularly Freemasonry, and especially in America. I was able to form a clear picture of the history of the various orders and the intent of their founders.

As I have pointed out, I became aware of a cold or secret war being waged within the Lodge space, mostly between two factions of lodge members in the Scottish Rite and York Rite. From this not always obvious conflict, I began to pay attention to various orders attached to Blue Lodge Freemasonry proper, as well as a close study of the origins of Freemasonry in America.

The first question that arises is: What is Freemasonry? There are some 70,000+ publications attempting to define and express the answer. But from a strictly utilitarian perspective, I would define Freemasonry as a system developed in the time of the Renaissance into the Enlightenment as a self-help program, originally in the form of Protestant mystical rites and ceremonies modified from extant Christian Mysteries and other Hermetic sources.

The next question concerns the History and origins of Freemasonry. When did Freemasonry begin? The official version of Craft Masonry says four Lodges agreed to "resume communication", which presupposes a former system prior to the official creation date of Freemasonry in 1717. What most people don't know is six Lodges actually met that fateful day at Apple Tree Tavern. Two Lodges didn't like what they heard at this meeting and left, and upon returning to their respective home Lodge spaces, they proceeded to destroy the records of their own archives-going back to time immemorial-and faded from history.

By 1725, the new form of English Craft Masonry established at Apple Tree Tavern by the four remaining Lodges had immigrated to the Continent, arriving in France to be embraced like nowhere else except maybe Germany. And as we have already mentioned, degree peddlers sprang up across Europe inventing hundreds of extra degrees, complete with fabricated false claims of lineage. After Chevalier Ramsey's legendary oration, occurring supposedly in the 1730's, Templar Masonry sprouted as a branch of the Craft; out of which bloomed the Rite of Perfection and Rite of Strict Observance and eventually the Scottish Rite, an order outside of Freemasonry, which is governed by a totalitarian hierarchy not unlike the Papacy itself with its College of Cardinals in the form of the Supreme Council 33rd of Inspector Generals.

The York Rite, on the other hand, in principle and practice completely democratic and members only serve in leadership roles for one year terms. All policies and actions voted on by majority rule. Though alas, it seems the governing bodies at the National level, and some State levels, have been infiltrated and overrun by agents of the Scottish Rite and other side orders. Many bureaucratic "councils of administration" have been formed to concentrate and consolidate power.

Always keep in mind, when one obligates themselves to the Scottish Rite they take a universal oath of fealty to the Supreme Council 33rd degree first and foremost above all others. We will return to the Supreme Council before we conclude but let us now look at the York Rite a bit closer. In its history we will see the shift in Ancient Craft Masonry which amounted to the usurpation of its authority by foreign outside interests represented by the Supreme Council of the Scottish Rite.

We have already mentioned the formation of Ancient Craft Masonry in America; how several Grand Lodge systems from Europe founded subordinate lodges in the Colonies, often times through "Sojourner Lodges"(soldiers stationed in foreign lands) which continued to meet regularly in Lodges wherever their base. As the sun never set on the British Empire the Crown spread masonry everywhere the imperium reached. America was not excluded from this action though, many Crowns of Europe had the same designs, and English Lodges were not the only ones formed in the New World; even so, in North America the Grand Lodge of England clearly dominated. In these early days Lodge traditions in Colonial America developed regionally and, as with all social institutions, the region's cultural identity set the standard.

It was from this early foundation that Ancient Craft Masonry was established. When The Revolution began, America declared independence from England in all ways, including the Grand Lodge System. The Royal Arch degree was also conferred, as well as the Knights of Malta and Knight of the Red Cross, at this same time period. By 1769 there were three Knights Templar dubbed in Boston: Brothers Paul Revere, William Davis, and the hero of the Battle of Bunker Hill, General Joseph Warren.

All these men fought at Bunker Hill. Sir Knight Davis devised the highly effective "barrel brigade", where oaken barrels were filled with mud and stone and rolled down on top of the approaching British soldiers. Legend has it General Warren was killed in the battle, his body discovered in a pile of corpses with a sword stuck in his side. The body was so badly mangled, in fact, Sir Knight Paul Revere had to confirm the silver work he had done on Warren's teeth to determine his identity.

One of the first Knights Templar Funeral Processions through the streets of Boston paraded the remains of General Warren after the Battle of Bunker Hill; wood plate engravings still exist today depicting the event. (A fraternal order named the Order of the Sword of Bunker Hill exists which reenacts this procession on flooring coverings spread out on the Lodge floor depicting the streets of colonial Boston commemorating this historic event. I joined the Dodge City, Kansas Chapter of the order of the Sword of Bunker Hill becoming one of the modern day Sons of Liberty during my time in the Blue Lodge.)

With the Revolution, and eventual independence of America, a new brand of Ancient Craft Masonry was modified from the English version by two key players in this history; Thomas Smith Webb and Jeremy Ladd Cross.

Thomas Smith Webb was made a Master Mason at Rising Star Lodge in Keene, New Hampshire in 1790; he is most recognized as the original innovator of the American (York) Rite of Ancient Craft Masonry, redesigning and elaborating the succession of Lodge, Chapter, and Commandery degrees by modifying these from the Prestonian Corpus-the body of work and lectures constructed by the English mason William Preston, one of the 18th century's intellectual leaders of Freemasonry, who ascertained that the purpose and mission of Masonry was to educate the members of the fraternity. From Preston, Webb learned and drew Masonic authority for his modifications.

Webb produced the first standardized set of American Freemasonic rituals; one key distinction being the excising of all monarchical references and deference. Webb traveled far and wide standardizing, then propagating, the American Rite throughout the Colonies and the early days of the Republic. His commitment to the Craft was clearly demonstrated by the fact that he actually died on the floor of the Lodge whilst doing courtesy ritual work.

His finest student and close protégé, Jeremy Ladd Cross, was made a Mason at St. John's Lodge in Portsmouth, New Hampshire in 1808. Cross had both a photographic, and phonographic, memory which served him well, both as ritualist and lecturer; he took up the mantle of the cause for American Craft Masonry, remaining active and in leadership in many concordant orders, as well as Freemasonry proper, for half a century. During the first ten years of peripatetic teaching, Cross propagated the work, ritual and lectures in a complete and beautiful system modified from Webb's innovations.

Most Masons would agree that Cross' own True Masonic Chart, or Hieroglyphic Monitor (1819)-the first of many books to be taken as the "standard" workbook-was perfected from the ritual work Webb developed for practice in Ancient Craft Freemasonry in America. He personally wrote and published monitors for all of the orders under the banner of the American Rite, especially the Cryptic Council Degrees or the Council of Royal and Select Masters work, which he delivered lectures on and sold while touring many lodges of America.

A booklet about Cross titled Jeremy Ladd Cross published and distributed by the General Grand Council of Cryptic Masons International tells us that for twenty years he lived in New York City publishing several editions of his monitors. He also kept a room devoted to the sale of his books and Masonic items; "…lodge and chapter decorations, jewels, and furniture, collars, etc…" of his own design. According to Robert Folger, Cross was "…the chief and most reliable dealer in masonic books and merchandise at that time…his character as a man and mason was unimpeachable there was no single man in the whole land more highly esteemed by the brotherhood".

Interestingly in 1851, Cross was persuaded to accept the post of Sovereign Grand Commander in the schismatic, or recently fabricated bodies of the Scottish Rite, and take the position as nominal head of the "Atwood" Supreme Council Northern Jurisdiction. An incarnation of the infamous Cerneau Council, it was a rogue Supreme Council empowered by the Grand Lodge of Louisiana and the Grand Orient of France.

Folger interviewed the nearly 70 year old Cross to obtain his consent to take the post, to which Cross responded by bringing forth his Patent (33rd Degree) which had laid dormant from the time of its issue, on June 24th, 1824 from the Supreme Council of AASR Charleston, South Carolina, and stated that he had never used it because of his attachment to the ritual and the principles of Ancient York Masonry, as well as the light opinion he had entertained of the so-called "Ineffable Degrees" of the Scottish Rite. Now an old man Cross, who had been educated in the Ancient York System and had labored earnestly through the years of his life to build it up, saw no other Masonry in the world but that particular form. He believed all else under the name of Masonry must be subservient and yield to the York Rite precedence in all things. He agreed to take the office if it was clear he could benefit Ancient York Masonry to which he was so much devoted.

He also made two other conditions to his consent to take the post:

1. It should be a fundamental law of the Supreme Council that none but Royal Arch Masons should be received up to the 16th degree.
2. That the remaining degrees (17-33) would be open only to Knights Templar.

Two years later Cross resigned from the post, never seeming to have officially functioned as Grand Commander. Albert Pike himself confirmed Cross' 33rd Degree patent genuine.

Let us now take a moment to consider Cross' own words with regards to the Scottish Rite.

In a short history of the 33rd Degree penned in 1852, he said, "…the Ineffable Degrees of Masonry are of modern origin. Most of them were created in France where 'the attachment of the French people for innovation and external finery, produced the most unwarrantable alterations upon the principles and ceremonies of the Order'…these dangerous innovations have not the smallest connection with the principles of ancient Freemasonry. They are unnatural excrescences formed by a warm imagination and fostered by the interference of designing men."

He spoke of the "purity" of Freemasonry as being contained in the first nine degrees and that Germany and France had been "…the prolific parent of a thousand devices… calculated to degrade the simplicity and beauty of our Society…with a view of gain, or gratifying that taste for the frivolous parade which is the natural companion of frivolous minds." He explains that numerous degrees had been invented and attached to the body of Freemasonry and that their creators would have them more exalted than Freemasonry in that: "…they are decorated with stars, and ribbons, and garters and other insignia, all calculated to mislead the weak, the frivolous and the vain; they are attended with all the pomp, and mystery, and solemnity which the imagination can invent…"

Speaking of the York Rite in America, he says, "…in this country Ancient Masonry, as used and taught in the first nine degrees since its first establishment, has existed in its pure, unsophisticated state…", and of the Scottish Rite "…the Ineffable Degrees are in no way connected with Ancient Craft Masonry, as practiced in our Blue Lodge, or the Chapter degrees…nor have they any connection with the Orders of Knighthood…as conferred in this country, in England, or in Scotland; yet they borrow largely of all the emblems and illustrations of Ancient Craft Masonry."

Cross traces the History of the Scottish Rite to the Scotch rite constitutions of October 25th 1762, at which point the King of Prussia was proclaimed its chief and given the titles of Sovereign Grand Inspector General and Grand Commander. The higher Councils and Chapters could not be opened without his presence, or that of a substitute appointed by him; apparently no provisions were established within the constitutions for a successor to the King as the highest ranking officer of the Rite.

It was for this reason, according to Cross' account, that the 33rd degree was established by the King of Prussia, and from those possessing this degree, the Supreme Council was formed; a body which then possesses all the Masonic rights and prerogatives formerly exercised by the King of Prussia. According to these early constitutions, not more than one Supreme Council can exist in each State (nation state) and it must be composed of nine members called Sovereign Grand Inspector Generals, at least five of whom must profess the Christian Religion.

That same year, in Berlin, the Grand Masonic Constitutions were ratified and proclaimed for the government of all Masonic bodies working the Rite of Perfection over the two hemispheres. They were transmitted to Stephen Morin, who had been appointed Inspector General for the New World in August 1761, by the Grand Consistory of Princes of the Royal Secret, convened at Paris under the Presidency of Chaillon de Joinville, Substitute General of the Order. Morin went on to America and appointed Moses Hays Deputy Inspector General, who then appointed Isaac Da Costa Deputy Inspector General for the State of South Carolina, who in 1783 established a Sublime Grand Lodge of Perfection in Charleston. Joseph Myers was appointed to succeed Da Costa after his death, by Hays. Myers appointed Solomon Bush Deputy Inspector for Pennsylvania, and Berend Spitzer for Georgia; confirmed at a Council of Inspectors in Philadelphia on the 15th of June, 1781. On the 1st of May, 1786, the grand Constitutions of the Supreme Council of the 33rd degree were ratified by the King of Prussia, by which the said prerogatives of the King and his Inspectors were deposited in a Council consisting of nine brethren in each nation.

An important point must be made here with regards to the King of Prussia, and any said power he might wield over Freemasonry anywhere, and the origins of what might be called the Prussian system of Social Control. As we pointed out earlier, the Prussian model of compulsion schooling was at least ideologically embraced by Horace Mann and New England Education System, and eventually nationwide. John Taylor Gatto's groundbreaking work in Dumbing Us Down and The Underground History of American Education continues to be cited as great source materials.

Let us examine a bit further, the history behind the Prussian "model" which the leaders of industry used as a foundation for American compulsion schooling, among other facets of our modern society. According to Wikipedia, "during the 13th century, the Old Prussians were conquered by the Teutonic Knights, and gradually assimilated over the following centuries. The former German state of Prussia took its name from the Baltic Prussians, although it was led by Germans who had assimilated the Old Prussians; the old Prussian language was extinct by the 17th or early 18th century. Prussia entered the ranks of the great powers shortly after becoming a kingdom and exercised most influence in the 18th and 19th centuries. During the 18th century it had a major say in many international affairs under the reign of Frederick the Great." [41]

Historian Thomas Babington Macaulay tells us, Frederick brought the concept of warfare to a whole new level, in a way that no other European power had before; governing his own kingdom "as he would govern a besieged town, not caring to what extent private property was destroyed or civil life suspended. The coin was debased, civil functionaries unpaid, but as long as the means for destroying life remained Frederick was determined to fight to the last." [42] Goethe said Frederick "saw Prussia as a concept, the root cause of a process of abstraction consisting of norms and attitudes, and characteristics which acquired a life of their own. It was a unique process, supra-individual, an attitude depersonalized, motivated only by the individual's duty to the State" [43]

Frederick William II, nephew of Frederick the Great, was no better. Under his rule, "the citizens of Prussia were deprived of all rights and privileges. Every existence was comprehensively subordinated to the purposes of the State and in exchange the State agreed to act as a good father, giving food, work, and wages suited to the people's capacity, welfare for the poor and elderly, and universal schooling for children." [44] In effect, this was the birthplace of the Nanny State, which offered a powerful opposition to the current industrial capitalism paradigm.

The social system in the small State of Prussia, in Northern Germany has been described as a "gigantic penal institution"; all state-approved, regimented and regulated even down to the architecture and the grid like structure of the street and buildings. The all too familiar attempts to purge society of undesirables-beggars, vagrants, Gypsies, et al, went into effect with the intent of turning Prussian society into "a 'huge automaton'…where scientific farming alternated with military drilling and state-ordered meaningless tasks" the sole purpose of which was to "subject the entire community to the experience of collective discipline… (It) had become a comprehensive administrative utopia. It was Sparta reborn… (sprung) out of the psychological emptiness which happens where…there is no other social and political life around which seems attractive or even safe … (In order) to bestow order and assistance on an unwilling population: to provide its clothing and food. *To schedule it.*" [45, 46]

This was Prussia. The King was not a just ruler, and certainly not the sort of example one would readily seek in the august halls of Freemasonry. And what sort of Masonic right and prerogatives would such a ruler demand and transfer to a Supreme Council established to contain said powers? Make no mistake about it, the modern members of the Scottish Rite are all too eager to claim connection, lineage, and authority to and from Frederick the Great of Prussia.

Back to Cross' short History. On February 20th 1788 a Grand Council of Princes of Jerusalem was opened in Charleston by Myers, Spitzer, and A. Forst-Deputy Inspector General for Virginia. In 1795, Colonel John Mitchell, appointed by Spitzer, replaced Myers on the Council. On May 31st 1801, the Supreme Council of the 33rd degree was opened with the grand honors of Masonry in Charleston, by John Mitchell and Frederick Dalcho, both Sovereign Grand Inspector Generals. Keeping in mind the method and standards employed to "communicate" all these supposed honors, rights, and powers already outlined in previous chapters, one can really not be sure how consistent or coherent any of these communications were.

According to Cross, this was the origin of the "Scotch rite" in the United States, of which there exists two Supreme Councils; one at Charleston (now Washington D.C.) and another in the city of New Orleans which eventually moved to New York.

A side note is made with reference to this other Supreme Council. In 1795, the Grand Orient of France established a Supreme Council of New Orleans while that portion of land was French Territory. After Jefferson "acquired" the territory and Louisiana became a State, a dispute immediately arose between the two Councils concerning supremacy. According to the 18th century constitutions, there should be only one Supreme Council per nation. Louisiana declared her date older than Charleston, while Charleston insisted she was first in America. Both Councils appealed their cases to the Grand Orient which chose to avoid the conflict. Charleston rejected the Grand Orient of France as ineffectual, and continued to denounce the Louisiana Council as illegal and spurious.

The Grand Orient, upon receiving word of Charleston's denunciation, immediately deputized Mr. Joseph Cerneau to form a Supreme Council in New York City, for the Northern Jurisdiction of America, in October 1807. Cerneau only served as Grand Commander for one year, but his infamy would live on in the Supreme Council of his name, and works such as one entitled "Scottish Rite Cerneau Wrong" would appear in time. Eventually, the Marquis De Lafayette would occupy the station of Grand Commander of the New York Supreme Council until his return to France. This Northern body of Supreme Council would, in 1851,-appoint Jeremy Cross its Grand Commander, empowered by his Patent issued from the Charleston Council in 1824.

In 1855, Jeremy Cross published an amazing little hardcover pocket book called The Masonic Textbook. Early in the work, Cross attempts to clarify some of his remarks which seem to have been misconstrued concerning Scottish Masonry in America and the formation of the York Rite. Some brothers seem to have taken Cross' comments to mean the York Rite was modified from the Scottish Rite, or what was then known as the Ineffable Degrees. The Scottish Rituals Cross referred to, being those performed by and under the Grand Lodge of Scotland which had chartered many lodges in colonial America known as "Scottish Lodges", and performing the ancient work in the same way for time immemorial.

Cross is adamant about clarifying the distinction here. He states in no uncertain terms that the Ancient and Accepted Rite, under that name, did not come into existence until 1802, and was reintroduced to Europe in 1804; and that the Scottish Rite-first officially introduced as such by Albert Pike-as clearly nothing more than a modification of the Rite of Perfection. In this explanation we are also informed that Morin, having been empowered as Inspector of the New World in 1761, had his powers recalled in 1766 "...as a consequence of misconduct after his arrival in the Caribbean"!

Cross concludes by telling us that, in the year 1802, the following notice appears in the minutes of the Grand Lodge of Scotland, relating to a circular letter addressed from the so-called Supreme Council of Charleston, "This year a circular letter was received from a Supreme Masonic body in America. The spirit of illumination which it breathed, and the supernumerary degrees, amounting to about fifty, which it authorized, were sufficient reasons for drawing down the contempt of Scottish Masons, whose honor it is to have preserved Free Masonry for many centuries in its original and simple form, and whose pride it shall ever be to transmit to the latest posterity the principles and ceremonies of their Order unpolluted and unimpaired." [47]

What more shall we say here? It seems clear to all involved that the "Ancient and Accepted Scottish Rite" system, which was first sent back to France after its initial American transformation in 1804, was an acknowledged *novelty* modified from the original 25 degree system of the Rite of Perfection, itself a modified invention. The York Rite, on the other hand, was forged in the early days of this great nation's founding; a homegrown evolution of original Colonial traditions, woven from a broad tapestry of several Ancient Craft Masonry traditions, primarily those of the British Isles.

Yet whenever we see an article or mainstream research paper, listen to or watch programs on mainstream media, we invariably hear from so-called "experts" supposed to represent the Fraternity of Freemasonry. Yet these same usual suspects, always listed as high ranking members of the Supreme Council and Scottish Rite, are speaking for Freemasonry proper. Why, and most importantly, *how* did this happen?

Returning again to Henry Coil's Freemasonry Through Six Centuries, he informs us that the "French Rite of Perfection, placed under the control of a self-constituted Supreme Council 33rd degree organized at Charleston, South Carolina in 1801…was returned to France in its new form by the Patent…issued in 1802…it was there both misunderstood and misused as the purported governing body, not only of the higher degrees, but also for the Symbolic Lodges, with the consequent demoralization of the whole of French Masonry…In the British Isles and the Colonies including America there was from the first a persistent belief in the primacy of Craft Masonry, the Royal Arch, Mark Master, and other additional degrees being accepted…in organization and government the institution remained democratic and the ancestry of the Fraternity was recognized to be of the commonality…a departure of this concept was the practice of placing a nobleman or prince at the head of the Grand Lodge.

"The French on the other hand conceived of Masonry as coming from the crusades and hence being a chivalric order, the "plebian" members of which ought to be content with an obscure position. Scots Masters were…deemed superior to and independent of the Masters of Symbolic Lodges thus constituting a ruling class…These Higher Grade Scots Masters did not pretend in any English-speaking countries to interfere with the exclusive control of Symbolic Masonry by Grand Lodges." [48]

Coil tells us that nothing much is known about the doings of the Southern Supreme Council from its inception in 1802 to 1844, in fact, little was to be known because it seems the Council made little or no effort to extend the Rite or expand its own influence, with most of the fragmentary records kept during this period having been lost or destroyed. Moses Holbrook became Grand Commander in 1826 and encountered the effects of the Anti-Masonic excitement generated by the Captain William Morgan controversy (a subject well known and too broad to address here) which almost resulted in the complete extinction of Freemasonry in America.

Dr. Albert Mackey was raised a Master Mason in 1841 and became Secretary General of the Southern Jurisdiction Scottish Rite in 1844, a position he held until his death in 1881. Coil informs us that, during most of that period Mackey occupied high offices in the York Rite. While Mackey is still known to this day as an authority on Freemasonry, with his famous lexicon and multiple volumes and revisions of his encyclopedia rotting on the shelves of every Lodge library in America, Mr. Coil points out that Mackey's "principle fault was his disposition to be dogmatic about theories which are unproved and some of which he afterwards renounced or greatly qualified...(and) it must be remembered that the first period of his writing was in the Age of Fable, prior to 1860, while the last 20 years were in the era of true historiographical research in which he himself joined...and discovered his earlier errors." [49]

Mackey's work was very influential, circulating across America in a time when the average Mason could not gather ample materials on Freemasonry to properly study the subject. Mackey's work provided easy source material, even if erroneous. Some of his mistaken notions about Freemasonry persist to this day as a result of Mackey's influence on the Craft. Coil makes one very remarkable point about Mackey's high office in the Scottish Rite which he held for many years, yet produced nothing on the subject of this Rite. With all the words he spared for Freemasonry, not one sentence was uttered in print concerning the Rite which would, one day, seem to hold Freemasonry in its grasp as Supreme Commander of its destiny. To complete the timeline of Mackey in this section, we should take a moment to highlight his relationship to one, Albert Pike; raised a Master Mason in 1850 Arkansas and Royal Arch Degree the same year, who in 1852-53 received Cryptic Degrees and was dubbed a Knight Templar in Washington D.C.

In 1853, Pike moved his law office to New Orleans, it was here Pike found the Scottish Rite and, one supposes, his first contact with the Order. It is suggested that Dr. Mackey communicated the 4th-32nd degrees of the Rite to Pike that same year, after both men travel to Charleston; Pike then took some of the rituals back to Arkansas with him. Two years later, we find Pike appointed by the Supreme Council to revise the rituals of the Rite, Pike was the only 32nd degree on a Council of 33rd degree Inspectors.

In 1857 he was elected an honorary 33rd, and the following year he became an active member of the Supreme Council in Charleston. By 1859, a mere eight years since this man approached the doors of a Blue Lodge, he was elected Sovereign Grand Inspector General and Grand Commander of the Supreme Council 33rd of the Ancient and Accepted Scottish Rite-the variation on the name of the Rite officially was established by Pike that year during the Grand Session of the Supreme Council-a position he held until his death in 1891.

Yet in Coil's informative history we find this quote from Albert Pike, assessing the Rite he "inherited" from Mackey, "I have said that the rituals of the degrees of the Ancient and Accepted Scottish Rite and those of the Rite of Perfection when I received them were worthless. I repeat it, excepting the Rose Croix only. They taught a man nothing that he did not already know before. They were not impressive in any way. No man of intellect and knowledge could regard them as." [50]

I would make note here of the remarkable resemblance of these words to those of the members of the Blue Lodge I joined, with regards to the York Rite, when queried! These are words, from the great Albert Pike himself, with regards to a collection of degree inventions, innovations, and modifications which should have rightly faded into the fog of time with the hundreds of others of their kin, yet this was not the case.

Somehow this seemingly insignificant side order, quietly coasting in the wake of the massive vessel that was Ancient Craft Masonry in America in the 19th century, ascended to a position of prominence and leadership in the Masonic Temple usurping several other Orders with equal or far greater seniority and authority to claim.

In the process of doing this it disabled the main corpus of Craft Masonry in America, the one Order with a true tradition and authority stretching back to before the Revolution.

6

THE WAR OF THE RITES

In the winter of 2007-2008, things were looking very promising for me and my little family. After years of working for the major cable companies, answering the phone calls of literally thousands of irate unsatisfied customers, I had secured a contracted position managing a much smaller call center. The job was gathering leads on prospective clients for independently licensed insurance agents in the field in desert towns across America's southwest. The entire operation had to do with government Medicaid and Medicare programs, most especially a supplemental program designed, in theory, to help cut the costs of overpriced medicines being prescribed to senior citizens at an obscene rate.

The job itself really seemed almost too good to be true for my situation, and as is often the case...it was. I was responsible for the production of "phone leads" from 10 call reps weekly. I was given my own office, overseeing a 15 station call center (also administrating the server network which was not part of the original offer). It was a modest salary with a weekly production bonus based on total production output from the call center. I was recruited for the position by the owner right off the call center floor after out producing the entire staff, including the top number earners in my first week.

What I did not realize upon hiring was I would also be expected to maintain and repair a very substandard "rigged-up" computer network server for the entire office, a real do-it-yourself handy man's nightmare. This extra responsibility was not properly compensated for within the salary package, but with promises of future growth and prosperity and the chance to be "the boss" on the floor, I went for it.

At the same time I had joined the local Blue Lodge and was advancing from the Second Degree of Fellow Craft to the Third Degree of Master Mason. Everything seemed right on track for the New Year to come. On January 2nd I showed up to work bright and early only to find the office door padlocked and the call center cleared out-it looked like it had been gutted. The owner of the call center had decided for the new fiscal year to close up shop clear out the office and run for the state border, thereby evading any potential prosecution for debt. What I did not know is he had moved the entire operation around the corner in the same office complex and set up shop to continue raking in leads until he left the state.

I was left with a broken contract trying to explain to a staff of 10 call reps why there would be no promised and expected bonus checks "…to start the New Year right!". In fact, there was no more "job" at all! And many of these people, I had personally recruited from other call centers on the promise of prosperity for all. Aside from the disgruntled personnel to contend with I also had a wife and 4 children to provide for in the middle of cold, harsh Midwestern winter. Upon closer investigation I discovered I was in fact ineligible for unemployment benefits as a contracted manager in an "at-will employment state"; we were left to fend for ourselves.

Now as Fellow Craft of the Blue Lodge, having gone through two ritual ceremonies being "made" an Entered Apprentice and "passed" to the degree of Fellow Craft, I was on the path to be "raised" to the sublime degree of Master Mason as soon as I proved "proficient" to advance to the next degree. Twice I had placed my life in the hands of indifferent strangers, twice I had knelt at the altar of Freemasonry and taken a sacred and solemn oath the keep the secrets of the Mysteries of Freemasonry, its signs of recognition and symbolic instructions. I had also sworn to fly to the general relief of any worthy brother in need. I was on the path of excellence in my mind and heart. I was answering a call to greater things, at the very least a greater understanding of all things.

"We are blind until we see that in the human plan, nothing is worth the making that does not make the man. Why build these cities glorious if man unbuilded goes? In vain we build the work unless the builder grows."
~Edwin Markham

Manly P. Hall recognized the inherent wisdom existing within Masonry, as written in his youth before he was even initiated into a Blue Lodge:

"The Eternal Quest-the average Mason, as well as the modern student of Masonic ideals, little realizes the cosmic obligation he takes upon himself when he begins his search for the sacred Truths of Nature as they are concealed in the Ancient and Modern Rituals. He must not regard his vows, and if he would not bring upon himself years and ages of suffering he must cease to consider Freemasonry solely as a social order only a few centuries old. He must realize that the ancient mystic teachings as perpetuated in the modern rites are sacred, and that powers unseen and unrecognized mold the destiny of those who consciously and of their own free will take upon themselves the obligations of the Fraternity. Freemasonry is not a material thing: it is a science of the soul; it is not a creed or doctrine but a universal expression of the Divine Wisdom.

The coming together of Medieval guilds or even builders of Solomon's Temple as it is understood today has little, if anything to do with the true origin of Freemasonry, for Masonry does not deal with personalities. In its highest sense, it is neither historical nor archaeological but is a divine symbolic language perpetuating under certain concrete symbols the sacred mysteries of the ancients. Only those who see in it a cosmic study, a life work, a divine inspiration to better thinking, better feeling, and better living with the spiritual attainment of enlightenment as the end, and with daily life of the true Mason as the means, have gained even the slightest insight into the true Mysteries of the Ancient Rites...")[52]

I carried these words close to my heart as I knocked upon the Lodge door. I understood myself to be beginning a powerful course of action; initiating transformative change in my very own consciousness. Now quite obviously everyone who petitions the Lodge for membership seeking the "Light of the Mysteries of Freemasonry" is not on the same quest as I. Nor would I suppose that this quest or path is the only way "up the mountaintop"-as I have already stated and will continue to do-there are literally millions maybe even billions of paths up to the mountaintop. Each one of us, whatever walk of life we tread, must find our own.

In order to prove proficient and advance to the next progressive degree, the Candidate must be instructed in an ancient catechism in the form of questions and answers recited from memory as close to verbatim- or word perfect-as humanly possible, to qualify as proficient. Training is received from a coach appointed by the Master and Secretary of the Lodge. I was being trained in my Masonic Catechism by a 90 year old Knight Templar, 33rd degree Sovereign Grand Inspector General (Honorary), and Secretary of the Lodge for almost 30 years. Although that same year he had stepped down as Secretary, he was still the unquestioned "decider" of all policy decisions and actions taken in the Lodge.

As a new member I had already eagerly expressed my interest in the Scottish Rite, in my ignorance of its true origins and any real authority it might possess. Being a new prospect, I was being groomed quite possibly to inherit the little Masonic Kingdom he held sway over in my new hometown. I met him weekly at a modest little bungalow he shared with his elderly wife in a retirement community. We would practice the "memory work" reciting the ritual parts over and over again until committed to memory. My coach was surprisingly adept at the work considering his age, he was able to recite most of the necessary rituals to open and close the Lodge, as well as the lectures and catechisms of all three degrees, all from memory and nearly word perfect!

Memory work strengthens the mind in preparation of the higher knowledge taken onboard during ritual initiation into progressive degrees. This "mouth to ear" fellowship also strengthens the bonds of the Mystic Tie between all lodge brothers.

We often discussed Freemasonry in very general terms. Among other things this brother communicated to me was his main contention that nothing a Mason needed was to be found within the York Rite. Even though he quite obviously took pride in being recognized as a Royal Arch Mason, and Knight Templar which were in fact York Rite Degrees-meaning he was a member of the York Rite! He insisted everything worthy of anyone's attention and commitment could be found exclusively in the Scottish Rite.

When I queried further with regards to the Holy Royal Arch Degree, and its importance to tradition in Ancient Craft Masonry, he claimed even the significant aspects of the Royal Arch were also contained within the Scottish Rite system of degrees. In fact, several of the small cabal of Scottish Rite brethren, who seemed ever-present and at the controls of every Masonic activity or function, espoused these same views publicly and one on one. I was very confused, puzzled, and eventually troubled by this. All of my "uninitiated" research had indicated things very much to the contrary. Regardless of all this, the brother was my coach and my personal liaison to the Lodge and as such I confided in him my financial troubles and woes with my sudden reversal of fortune after the New Year-to which I received a cold detached response.

I sensed a distinct disturbance in his minimal reaction-the way he bristled when the subject came up. But I did formally make application to the Lodge through this brother for temporary relief from immediate financial hardship. We were in great distress it was the middle of winter and I could only find under-employment which was not making the ends meet. At this time I was informed by this brother that the Lodge was not accustomed to having to actually provide such relief to a member even

65

though every member in the Lodge takes a sacred oath (on the Bible or other appropriate substitute Sacred Volume of the Law) upon joining to fly to the general relief of any worthy brother making application for such need.

What I did *not* know at the time was my home lodge had made some interesting and meaningful financial moves in the ten to fifteen years before I joined. The beautiful Temple downtown where I had my amazing visionary experience with the Sun, the Moon, and the red-tailed hawk was no longer even owned by the lodge, they had sold it for a fraction of its worth, to one of the most prosperous businessmen in town. It was eventually leased to a post-modern non-denominational evangelical church, while the Masonic orders were left to lease a business office space at $5,000 dollars a month in a five year contract.

When I queried those involved who were still living, they claimed they were convinced by the core Scottish Rite cabal that the Temple "...was too far gone to repair, and beyond help..."; thousands of dollars in custom oil-painted stage backdrops depicting the various Masonic scenes and themes abandoned, along with an impressive balconied performance area, and full size pipe organ-such a shame. And there was much more to the story.

The money that was banked after the Temple sale was being slowly eaten away by the new monthly lease payments for the lodge space, to be used by all the Masonic Orders along with all the usual operating costs. All this in the middle of a sharp decline in not only new membership but the resignation of existing members as well as more and more suspensions and expulsions for non-payment of dues, and simply death of old members. The economic "recession" only made matters worse for the Lodge and various concordant orders. The exchange I had with my Masonic coach generated a palpable amount of shame, but I was desperate to provide for my family in the middle of winter and convinced the Lodge was there to help I therefore persisted in my request for assistance to which my coach-visibly disquieted-replied, "I'll see what I can do."

In the eleventh hour, when all hope seemed lost and we seemed doomed to shut-off and possible eviction, I was offered "a loan" of $650.00, the exact amount to cover rent.

Called to the brother's humble home again, I was handed a check issued from something called "The Scottish Rite Almoner's Fund", with my coach and one other from the Lodge Scottish Rite Cabal as signatories.

I was told in no uncertain terms: "This is a *loan*. We need the money back in the fund as soon as possible. We could get our butts in a whole lot of trouble with *others* for pulling a fast one here…" I was apprehensive hearing this, for what I had originally thought was going to be the gift of relief I had applied for, was now "a loan" with pressure to return upon it. I had no idea that the so-called Almoner's Fund was a charitable fund administered by the local Scottish Rite Valley, *not* the Blue Lodge which I thought I was applying to for relief. Also this fund was not by any means established for *loans* to anyone, under any circumstances. It was a charitable fund to offer relief to needy applicants with no expectation of the money being paid back!

I knew none of this and of course felt caught by the short hairs. I would have agreed to almost anything to get the rent paid. I had every intention of honoring the agreement, though at the moment it was difficult to imagine repaying any debt, being unable to cover the costs of living. The next six months was a span of under-employment up until the housing bubble burst and the most severe financial crisis since the Great Depression took full effect on America. I made a few payments to my coach over the next few weeks and months, also advancing to the third degree of Master Mason in the Lodge.

All went well in this fashion until I was approached by several other brothers in the Lodge, the "Guardians of the Grail"-as I have referred to them in previous pages of this work-who made me aware of the war between the Rites; a secret, information cold-war. Both a political and ideological struggle, that seemed all but lost, by the York Rite the true custodians of the tradition of Ancient Craft Masonry in America. What these other brothers gently suggested to me was that all was not what it seemed in the Lodge, that brotherly love and friendship did not prevail but was, in fact, strained. Certain key facts were being actively and deliberately suppressed with regards to what Ancient Craft Masonry really was, and what the Scottish Rite was. From here on everything changed.

What these other brothers shared with me explained why I felt so troubled by the views expressed by my coach and his cronies. It may help to make some points here with regards to the organizational structure, legally and traditionally, of subordinate Blue Lodges in America. While the Master of the Lodge is the unquestioned leader-whose word and will are law-it is only a temporary appointment. Most lodge systems hold yearly elections to fill the chairs of the various key officers of the Lodge for carrying out the business of the Order for the year. Some Lodges elect the Master for a three year term but most elect for only one.

These days, the average Brother Mason, with little or no Lodge experience, is prematurely advanced through the line of officers by jumping over, or skipping, chairs in the line; as the need always seems to arise, with the severe decline of membership and participation in lodges. He is therefore little equipped to properly execute the duties of the office of Master without exceptional aptitude, leadership skills, and assistance. The assistance he receives comes usually from the Secretary's chair just south of his own in the Lodge. By the time he will be accustomed to the role, the year term is up and the Lodge is on to the next new elected Master.

The Secretary of any Lodge Chapter, Council or Commandery in a Masonic Temple is by far the most important single position to ensure smooth or difficult sailing in the regular business-which means everything from organizing a public dinner and address, to deciding on a monthly meeting agenda with the current Master, to any number of minutiae of details, factors, and decisions that need to be arranged and accomplished each month, in a properly functioning lodge. The Secretary knows all the finer demographical details on every member-having reported such details back to the respective Grand body governing the organization within whose jurisdiction every subordinate lodge operates.

Every detail that can be gathered, recorded, filed, and stored on state-of-the art database software has become the standard of most Fraternal Orders in America. All activities and functions of, or related to, a Lodge are pre-approved by the Secretary. All outside communication with the Lodge passes through the Secretary's hands in order to be presented to the brethren, as well as all petitions for Candidate applications, honors and awards for brother lodge members. In true fact, nothing happens in a Lodge that the Secretary doesn't know about and hasn't already approved and organized.

Most Masters of the Lodge rely solely on the Secretary's judgment and guidance during their short term in office, rubber-stamping whatever the Secretary proposes. A good lodge Secretary, such as my coach, could sit in the Secretary's Chair for years, even decades, as no one wanted the thankless job with so many details to cover; and in this capacity, effectively rule over a lodge for almost thirty years which, as it turns out, is what happened in the decades prior in my new home Lodge-or "Mother Lodge", as a home lodge is known.

For the sake of this discourse, and to avoid as much unnecessary legal actions as possible, we will continue to generalize and identify said individuals and specific civic municipal organizations in generic terms. That said, with closer examination of the records, histories, and accounts placed in the archives of "Lodge X", which I joined on Veteran's Day 2007, I found many interesting facts and truths. Lodge X, like many in America, was part of a small confederacy of concordant fraternal orders and organizations, all using the same "Masonic Temple Center" as their respective lodge space during their individual business meetings throughout each month; each Order, in effect renting the space, which was applied to cover the costs of operating and maintaining the Center.

At the beginning of the 20th century, Lodge X had joined the four other Orders affiliated with Freemasonry- the Order of the Eastern Star, the White Shrine, the York Rite, and the Scottish Rite-in building the local Masonic Temple Center.

A pamphlet I rescued from the trash bin of my "home" Lodge-printed for a 1924 dedication ceremony of the magnificent stone Temple downtown, where I'd had my hermetic vision-recounts the history of the Temple construction in the early 1900's.

It seems, according to this pamphlet, that in the latter part of the 19th century the Scottish Rite had been making inroads on the Masonic and fraternal population and had begun designs on building a "Cathedral" for the Scottish Rite, and the other Orders, to use and better serve the growing membership they were experiencing.

This apparently seemed disquieting to enough members of the other Orders affiliated with Freemasonry in the area, including the 2 Blue Lodges under the Ancient Free and Accepted Masons banner, that they responded by forming a Masonic Temple Corporation with the expressed purpose of "raising funds and constructing a Temple Center to serve all the Fraternities". The reason, explicitly stated in the pamphlet history in the form of a public address at the dedication ceremony, was to prevent the Scottish Rite from taking over Masonry in the city and, by default, taking a leadership role over all the concordant orders operating there!

A beautiful structure was raised in the center of commerce and community on the main street of downtown, complete with stone pillared columns adorned with Masonic and Egyptian iconography. It still stands like a monument to the Mysteries-truly like an ancient light in modern times. The funds to build this structure were raised by selling off shares of stock in the Masonic Temple Corporation to the members of all the various Orders involved. A set number of shares were created, and sold, to all takers with 100 shares leftover unsold upon completion of the building and stored in the Temple office safe.

When members who purchased shares passed away, if they still held the stock (often members sold or donated back their shares to the various Orders they belonged to), it reverted back to the Temple Corporation, though the shares were usually dropped off at the Temple office and placed in the common safe used by all of the organizations. Often times, the particular Order a deceased member was most active in would get the shares placed in their coffer. It seems a bit "fuzzy" how this all worked out.

Another note regarding the organizational structure of Fraternal Orders: each organization has its own Secretary, or Recorder, keeping the records and maintaining the archives of the Order. In a shared environment such as a Masonic Center, many hands have access to records, archives, secure files, and safes or vaults. Over time things get moved, shifted around, misplaced, or lost altogether. For example the hundred-odd leftover shares, unsold from the building of the Temple, in the office somehow ended up shifting from the Temple holdings to the Scottish Rite coffers.

The Secretary of the Lodge could also be Secretary of other Orders in the same office, sharing the same spaces. Such individuals would be in a position to intercept all shares returning from deceased member's families-as well as other rare items like books, regalia, and other valuable paraphernalia. Which is, in fact, what seems to have happened over decades. There were strange transactions as well recorded in the official registers, such as shares of the Masonic Temple Corp. stock, being *paid* to the Scottish Rite for "courtesy work"-an unprecedented practice, in that courtesy work by definition is given for free as a courtesy it is never charged for! And for that matter the Scottish Rite would never be in a position to offer work to any other Orders, especially the Blue Lodges of Ancient Craft Masonry-in that once again for the record; the Scottish Rite is *not* Freemasonry in no way shape or form except illegally and irregularly! This action constitutes fraud especially considering what happens next on this tale of one (out of numerous cities and towns in America) Masonic Temple Center.

As stated briefly above, 70 odd years after the Masonic Temple X was dedicated, the Scottish Rite-in a clear-cut power move-was somehow allowed to assume controlling interest of the Masonic Temple Corporation, following an audit of the Temple holdings, which determined the Scottish Rite Valley somehow held the majority of existing shares of stocks issued. Over the years, by hook or by crook, they had gathered and amassed all the shares floating out there by the means described above.

With this newly held control, the Rite next moved to sell the Temple property to a local business developer who owned the largest real estate interest in the city, the whole deal brokered through the then-retired Lodge Secretary, predecessor to my coach who was also a high-ranking officer in the Scottish Rite Valley, effectively removing a valuable piece of historical property (owned outright by everyone!) from the combined hands of the Masonic Orders, and replacing it with an uncanny 5-year lease on a commercial office-far removed from the foot traffic of downtown-for $5,000 a month, only slightly accommodating with many concessions made. This business decision slowly liquidated the Fraternal Orders combined cash and bond accounts earned from the sale of the Temple property for a fraction of its true worth.

And when I personally queried all the living members involved in the decisions made, members who actually voted to sell the Temple they loved, why they thought this would be a right and proper action, I was informed by all the same rote catechism-like response that "the building was too far gone... too far run down to be maintained...", the costs to repair and restore the building were deemed too much to even consider. Instead it was considered more equitable for all to sell off the actual valuable asset, divide up the profits, and then proceed to drain all the funds paying the costs of a commercial lease on office space and all the extra costs this generates.

What I would eventually discover through my research and private investigation is this same action had been, or was being, taken in jurisdictions all over America. Story after story in the news can be found with the same reports and outcomes. The end result over and over again: the local Scottish Rite leadership would assume control of all Lodge activities through infiltration; all decisions would slowly shift to be only favorable to them; which would naturally lead to the other Orders being disempowered and beholden to the Scottish Rite leadership, even though it had no authority to control anything Masonic, let alone the various other fraternal orders.

As one would expect, the effects of all this have been very demoralizing to the majority of members wherever this occurs. This 'Master Plan', perpetrated over and over again and again, the play is the same. And meanwhile the only the Grand Master, the public face of

Freemasonry, or one of his representatives-of any given jurisdiction, has the legal authority to speak publically for Freemasonry. On television channels like the History Channel, Discovery Channel, National Geographic Channel, and the silver screen it is always represented en masse by the Scottish Rite.

The spokesperson interviewed, and considered an expert, is invariably a 33rd degree, in his little white bell-hop cap-itself a direct rip-off of the York Rite Templar Order's red cap which accompanies a white mantle adorned with a red cross, and alternative to the "Class A" paramilitary black uniform with peacock feathered chapeau worn by Masonic Knights Templar. A further point to make is that I have *never* seen a man identified simply as an Ancient Craft Mason interviewed, or more importantly, an exclusively York Rite Mason asked for his opinion.

And so it seems from humble itinerant degree peddling beginnings, gradually, then more abruptly with the Civil War, key operatives of this innovation assumed leadership roles, eventually calling the shots within the age-old Colonial Pre-Revolutionary Fraternal orders with origins tracing back to the British Isles of time immemorial, thereby preceding said modern inventions in history and authority.

And still the question hangs in the air, hardly answered: Why? And *how* did this, by all definitions fraudulent and foreign, *novelty* system of esoteric degrees-loosely based on Masonic traditions and rituals-gain such a footing, such traction with the Fraternal Orders of America and the world? The simplest and easiest explanation it would seem is slowly, but surely: one Freemason at a time.

7

THE LAZY MAN'S PATH TO ENLIGHTENMENT

Whether you realize it or not, in this work so far, we have already revealed and reviewed some of the biggest and most powerful secrets of Freemasonry in general. Though it seems very few have yet to recognize these as such, because the truth often has so little bite without clear and proper discernment, as well as a bit of drama. People want hype and sensationalism, they want theatrics. But still the question remains: What does it matter what we know? Why does it matter at all?

It has continued to amaze and mystify me how the Scottish Rite gained such power in America, and it would seem, the world. The subtle yet constant rise to power and prominence is remarkable, in that Freemasonry is a system rife with guardians and custodians, jealously "protecting" the Fraternity from innovations and modifications. It seems impossible that such a trivial and novel system would be so successful and gain such influence.

The biggest secrets I have revealed in this work thus far, not only impact the true state of the Fraternal Lodge systems in America today at the very least, but also represent clear cut examples of the kind of misinformation and disinformation at play in all facets and levels of our lives as a social species; which serve to shape and sculpt reality as well as dictate policy and tradition to all no matter how faulty, flawed, or counterfeit. As a matter of policy and fact, error as an ideal seems preferred for its discordant, dystopian impact on awareness, which offers its own demoralizing "reward".

I have illustrated that Ancient Craft Masonry as presented here is, at its core, a "self-help", self-guided, educational system for individual and group spiritual development-a task which many great men and women have devoted their lives to throughout human history. It is no small feat to accomplish, indeed. We all struggle at different levels of growth and advancement on this path. To many this may seem unachievable, and, for many of them it may be.

When an Aspirant Candidate enters the august halls of Freemasonry and stands upon the checkerboard pavement, beholding the

Lodge edifice in full glory, it sparks something deep within; a genetic memory which ignites the binding line connecting the Brotherhood of The Mystic Tie to the electrical fabric of space/time reality, and to all individual initiates. This spark may hopefully inspire the most zealous brothers to truly pursue the seven liberal arts of the Trivium and Quadrivium combined: Grammar, Logic, Rhetoric, Astronomy, Music, Geometry, and Architecture. This is a life-long study which would surely increase one's general intelligence aptitude, but again, this is a huge undertaking requiring disciplined will and determination.

The vocation the Brother Knight Mason is called to is a long apprenticeship; seven years of hard work in the symbolic "quarries of the spirit", from Initiate Apprentice to Fellow of the Craft, where the education really steps-up. After a "Master"-piece is created, complete with a unique individual Master's Mark, the Brother is made a Master of the Lodge (Magister Templi), and maybe, eventually, *the* Master of the Lodge; sitting in the center chair of three in the East. Adhering to the proper order of progression in Ancient Craft Masonry in America, where every Grand Lodge has a slightly unique tradition with regards to all the degrees available, he continues to advance, educating himself and gaining knowledge all the while.

In the York Rite degree sequence, the Most Excellent Master degree must be received by the Aspirant in order that he might be advanced to the Sublime Degree of the Holy Royal Arch. The Most Excellent Master degree commissions Brother Companions by sacred vow to bring further light to Masons in Masonry, sharing the knowledge and wisdom they have and will gather with all Brethren. This charge is no small undertaking, it is a sacred commission.

What is the knowledge and wisdom gathered and how? And most importantly why bother at all? To answer these and other questions in the same realm of thinking we turn to an English scholar and Mason, Walter Leslie Wilmshurst, who lived from 1867-1939. In 1927 he wrote a powerful and useful little book called, The Meaning of Masonry. I often wonder if this book got lost under the radar at the time in America, what with the Great Depression kicking off and such. Even to this day it remains overlooked and undervalued; as a matter of fact, you can purchase a hard cover copy online today for about ninety-nine cents! Let not the perceived lack of monetary value of this book dissuade you dear reader from its impact and import, this book does as its own forward promises; it "discloses the real purpose of modern Freemasonry and clearly states the true body of teaching and practice concerning the esoteric meanings of the Masonic ritual" [53]

Returning now to the question of why bother with such an arduous task as self-improvement through spiritual growth and all that entails, we will consider what Wilmshurst offers up as reason. He makes it very clear that, in his day, an increasing number of Brethren sensed Freemasonry enshrined something deeper than they had been able to understand, with no good guidance. He also states in no uncertain terms that all matters such as dates, particulars, historical changes and developments, etc. are all subordinate to what is most important to the Brethren of the Craft; the knowledge of the spiritual purpose of the Order.

Wilmshurst tells us, the vital secrets of Freemasonry might as well be "shouted from the housetops…", as they would mean little or nothing to those unqualified or unprepared to recognize, or identify with, the knowledge contained therein. The uninitiated person is unready to unpack and take on board the wisdom encoded within the system of Freemasonry and incorporate it into their habitual thought and conduct. Not incapable, merely unprepared. He tells us that true initiation awakens the individual to an order and quality of life other than previously experienced.

We know that "initiation" means a new beginning, a break-away from old patterns of approach to reality and life. It is an entrance upon a new and intensified path, with deepened self-knowledge, understanding, and virtue; the initiate turns away from the popular culture which defines the ideals of the day. The initiate has the conviction that those ideals of popular culture lack true substance and are, but, mere shadows and temporal substitutions for the eternal reality that lay beneath.

For Wilmshurst it was clear that buried deep, hidden at the center innermost part of our souls, genuine secrets of the universe were concealed. All that was initially required of an Aspirant was a strong enough desire to learn the secret mysteries of his own being. As with all spiritual work he must "divest" himself of all prejudice thoughts or preconceived notions of the world and reality, assuming instead "a childlike meekness and docility", surrendering his understanding to the reception of a whole different set of truths, often novel and unexpected.

He understood, perhaps better than most, that Masonry was designed as an instrument of Initiation which teaches self-knowledge and transformation of consciousness. What is required of one who aspires to achieve such goals is the utter and complete laying aside of every other kind of knowledge and pursuing a long, strenuous, and difficult path. By his own admission, "the wisest and most advanced of us is perhaps still but an Entered Apprentice at this knowledge however high his titular rank…" [54]

As already stated, Wilmshurst was convinced of a secret path of life, other than that which we normally tread. For him the ritual was the vehicle, behind its more obvious symbolism there exists the framework of a process of initiation into a higher path of life, where we might learn the secrets and mysteries of our being and the universe around us.

He was also just as aware of the decline of Freemasonry, that it was already endangered in his time and that the members of the Order lacked real education of what the underlying philosophy of Freemasonry truly was, diverted from its original purpose. Whilst noble in gesture, the fact that the "initiating instrument" had been refitted to serve the charitable and philanthropic agendas of more socially motivated men, all these activities serve only to alienate the brethren from the true purpose of Ancient Craft Freemasonry as we present it here. In general, a true Mason must assume the posture of one who is spiritually poor and in darkness, content to renounce all temporal riches in pursuit of greater understanding of the mysteries of his own nature and those of the universe.

Without understanding of the deeper meaning and true purpose of its Rites and philosophy to translate its symbolism, Masons would inevitably mistake "shadow for substance…secularizing what was designed as a means of spiritual instruction and grace." [55] All through his book Wilmshurst describes a process of intense learning, a truly arduous task, a herculean effort, to transcend the social imprinting of a lifetime and invite transformative change into our very consciousness; which is at the root and heart of all spiritual systems. That's the plain and simple truth of it and it all amounts to very hard work on one's self.

Among the hundreds of Orders and Rites originally concordant to Freemasonry, there exists the Ancient Order of Druids in America, currently administered by Grand Arch Druid John Michael Greer; an amazing individual, prolific writer and thinker, as well as Brother Mason and Magickal Practitioner. I have had the honor and pleasure of interviewing Mr. Greer several times for my weekly radio broadcast The Middle Chamber on American Freedom Radio. He has written several extremely useful books for understanding my approach to all that has been discussed. A detailed list of these books can be found in the bibliography of this present volume. For the record, the AODA is no longer strictly concordant upon Freemasonry, in that membership in Freemasonry is no longer a prerequisite for membership in the AODA and women *are* allowed in the Order of Druids, while women are still archaically forbidden in Freemasonry.

I was always drawn to the Druid approach, probably because of my cultural heritage, and when I realized the Ancient Order of Druids was Masonic in origin I was very excited. The Ancient Order of Druids in America, founded in1912, is a branch of the Ancient and Archeological Order of Druids, which was founded in England in 1874 by the Mason, and Rosicrucian, Robert Wentworth Little. This English Order had close ties to esoteric circles within British Masonry including, obviously, the SRIA or Society of the Rose and Cross in England as well as the Hermetic Order of the Golden Dawn. Many notable Fraters were also Druids, and even Winston Churchill was a member of the AAOD.

Many Druid Orders including the United Order of Druids (UOD), trace their common origin back to the Ancient Druid Order with a traditional founding date of 1717, a few months after the founding of the first Masonic Grand Lodge of England (legend has it this happened in the very same Apple Tree Tavern) indicating the clearly close ties between Freemasonry, Rosicrucianism, and Druidry. Grand Arch Druid, Greer, has been instrumental in reorganizing and revising the Ancient Order of Druids in America (AODA a descendent of the AAOD) their teachings and curriculum in a very remarkable way. With decades of practice and experience in several other esoteric and magickal orders, such as the Hermetic Order of the Golden Dawn, Greer brings a focus and clarity to the practice which is learned, dynamic and very productive.

As of this writing Greer has produced a new work titled: The Celtic Golden Dawn, which combines Druidry with the Ceremonial Magick of the Hermetic Order. The book has spawned an online initiatory order as well.

I myself joined another occult correspondence school, right after joining the Masonic Lodge in 2007, called the Builders of the Adytum or, the BOTA, founded by another brother Mason and former member of the Golden Dawn, Paul Foster Case. Case created a system in the BOTA where he excised all Enochian, Goetic, and otherwise "questionable" (by his standards), magickal material from the curriculum of the Golden Dawn and streamlined it into a system which he began selling by mail-order in the 20's.

The BOTA continues to educate people to this day, and is a great introduction course in Occult fundamentals and philosophies. But the

Order of the Druids offers a more intense training and practice, as well as an Earth-based spiritual approach, all within the lodge structure of the western fraternal traditions.

One point to make is I have determined through extensive research and practice, and many hours of interviews with such luminaries as Master Lon Milo Duquette on the subjects of the Enochian and Goetic operations that both approaches have useful and productive applications. These powerful systems of self-transformation are often dismissed and avoided by other Magi for no real definite or substantial reasons other than prejudice, bigotry, and remnants of religious ignorance.

I self-initiated into the AODA during the Spring Equinox 2010 at dawn, in my mother's backyard, in the middle of a circle of standing stones next to her goldfish pond. After 3 years of intense study and practice, which included planting a tree (Birch), stewarding it for those 3 years, and keeping an extensive journal of all activities, research, and progress as well as many other requirements including discursive meditation and regular ritual and ceremony practice, I advanced from Candidate Initiate to Druid Apprentice 1st Degree in 2013, near the Winter Solstice. There are two more degrees which require 5 years total to advance, Candidate Initiate only required a minimum of 1 year.

Nonetheless the experience has been rewarding and enriching without equal. Simultaneously, the work has been strenuous and intense at times. Here we've provided just an example of what might be involved in truly educating oneself in the Western Mystery Traditions, within and without Freemasonic systems. All these spiritual development systems require varying degrees of effort and commitment. The tasks are not easy which leads one on the path to true enlightenment.

Herein lies the crux of the matter, why would any man of the mid-19th-20th century and beyond, already strapped for time and resources more and more each day, his attention called to greater and more lucrative things; why would such a man assign himself the tasks as described above, when there exists another way, an easier path, a "lazy" way out? The self-respecting modern, or modernizing, man would already feel entitled, if not qualified, to the greatness he aspires with passion and zeal! Should he have to toil and struggle, with something so seemingly unrewarding materially beyond its title, when he might instead simply attend a one day class or even simply collect his mail and receive 32 or 33 degrees, complete with a "princely" title and fancy gold-sealed certificate identifying him as such? And in fact we know that hundreds of thousands, perhaps even millions, of men did just this and do still to this day. Most don't know any better.

What seems the most likely explanation for the rise of the Scottish Rite, within the American Ancient Craft Masonry system, is simply convenience and good marketing. It was far easier for "progressive" American men, or in some cases high-ranking government and business leaders, to attend a one day class of receive extravagant looking certificates and patents by mail, than to commence real spiritual transformation from within. If the general populace of the organization is unaware of the truth and the substance behind the lofty claims of invented rites and orders, they will perceive the face value as fact, never suspecting the contrivance foisted upon their awareness.

I also agree with Wilmshurst's declaration regarding the absurdity of thought that such a vast organization like Freemasonry would be here merely to teach grown men of the world symbolic and emblematic interpretations of a few builders tools, as well as impress the most elemental of virtues that every child learns throughout their adolescence, along with the simple principles of morality taught in every church and religion. What remains, then, is an enquiry as to what would be worthy of being called a science or art within Freemasonry, and for each seeker to ascertain what those "mysteries" are to which one is promised the reception of? What is Freemasonry capable of teaching us? We conclude from the materials reviewed thus far that the true purpose of teaching the "Mysteries" is imparting to suitable and prepared minds certain truths of human life, certain instructions about divine things, about humanity's nature and destiny.

The enlightened vision that Wilmshurst gives us truly educates us with insight into our individual condition; "the lodge (is)…a sacramental figure of oneself and the mechanism of personal consciousness, opening the lodge in the successive degrees, implies the ability to expand, open up and intensify that consciousness in three distinct stages suppressing the normal level applicable to ordinarily mundane affairs…". [56]

As he understood it, a "vortex in the mental and psychical atmosphere" was created with the assemblage of persons working in concert of form and intent, and that a sort of tension is generated by the collective energy of thought and will which intensifies progressively through the degrees, leaving a permanent effect on the Candidate. All this induces a favorable mental and spiritual rapport between the Candidate, his guides, and those other initiates who have already passed through the veils to the path of enlightenment.

The preparation of the Candidate is of utmost importance. This point cannot be stressed enough. A Candidate properly exposed to ritual initiation has experienced intense mental stimulation; his perceptibility has been charged and permeated with potent ideas and influences transmitted through the craftsmen working the ritual. [57] There is an "eternal language of the gods" encoded within the signs and symbols of the Mysteries. This language speaks to our individual awareness, penetrating into the core consciousness within us all and bridging the abyss between, if only briefly, with profound impact.

The briefest review of tools and techniques employed in the Mysteries illustrate that the secret power of the Mysteries resides within the signs symbols, and emblems and their proper use. Vocals sounds, physical acts such as yoga, and mental intentions have always been employed to generate a dynamic spiritual force within; an intentional, concentrated atmosphere with the desired effect of "attaining stability of mind, control of emotions and thoughts, and to acquire interior stillness and harmony with all", that we might then unweave the veil after veil of illusory notions we maintain, concerning our real nature and the true nature of life, all the while keeping in focus the goal of enlightenment which compels us.

Of course all this depends on what the individual candidate intends on achieving through initiation. Intention, as always, lays the foundation of what we will experience when inviting this sort of transformative change into our consciousness. There is yet another course of action available to the newly made Master Mason, with regards to what path he would tread aside from the Lazy man's path of a one day class or simply receiving a certificate in the mail, as well as the true quest we have described above.

It remains a testament to this author's optimism that the present work exists. For this other path we speak of is the hardest to resist for many men it seems.

There resides within Freemasonry proper an overly expressed misunderstanding with regards to the official declaration of the United Grand Lodge of England, after the great compromise between the Moderns and Antients, or Ancients, in 1812-13, which allowed people to ignore the complete system of Ancient Craft Masonry in favor of an abridgement. From one of the original articles regarding the union of the two Grand Lodges (Modern and Ancient) of England, dated Dec. 1st 1813, it reads:

"It is declared and pronounced that pure Ancient Masonry consists of 3 degrees, and no more, viz: those of the Entered Apprentice, Fellow Craft, and the Master Mason (also including the Sublime Order of the Royal Arch). But, this article is not intended to prevent any Lodge or Chapter from holding a meeting in any of the degrees of the Orders of Chivalry, according to the Constitutions of said Orders."

The first detail which arises in the American Masonic mind when he reads the Sublime Order of the Royal Arch, included in the roll of degrees, is that in order for a Master Mason to qualify for the Royal Arch Degree he must first be made a Mark Master, Past Master, and Most Excellent Master; all of these degrees are contained within the York Rite system as perquisites of being exalted to the Sublime Degree of Royal Arch, which would effectively bring the tally to seven degrees; which can be thought of as the necessary progression to receive the complete Ancient Craft Masonry system.

Of course, the Cryptic Degrees, amounting to an 8th and 9th degree, and the Orders of Chivalry-which contains the three Orders of Malta, the Illustrious Red Cross, and Temple (Templar) Knights, already contained within the York Rite system-can only add to the splendor and pageantry of the Fraternal Lodge Systems experience. These "extra" degrees, bringing the total number to 12 within the York Rite, simply further the education and inspiration available to the individual aspirant in a consistent line with the teachings contained within Ancient Craft Masonry.

The declaration made by the United Grand Lodge of England or UGLE does not disqualify the York Rite and its' Orders-on the contrary it actually allows for it! Yet many Masons use the UGLE's statement cited above to justify their incomplete advancement through the whole system of Ancient Craft Masonry in America. They settle instead for the initial three degrees of the Blue Lodge and parrot the mantra that Freemasonry is "only the three degrees and no more!"

One must consider the politics within the quote from the article above. If nothing else, what remains clear is the Grand Lodge of England's desire to be the premier Grand Lodge of authority with regards to any and all things Masonic. And this goal was exceedingly accomplished. One clear and obvious way of doing this would be to modify the system of Freemasonry, effectively limiting or abridging the development of the Initiate within. By "dividing and halving", the progression system of Ancient Craft Masonry which resulted in spreading it out over two distinct Grand Lodge systems with a palpable rivalry-in and of itself rooted in the Grand Lodge of England's very apparent power move in 1717-when it declared itself the original and only "regular and lawful" form of Freemasonry, to the exclusion of such pre-existent traditions as the Scottish and Irish Grand Lodge systems which clearly did exist before 1717!

This is not the first time the obvious truth was ignored in favor of political expediency and it would certainly not be the last. The Grand Lodge of England clearly had, and has, its own agenda. And like a "three-card Monty" game of bait and switch, the "Queen" of Ancient Craft Masonry must be closely followed. In this instance we think of the Queen as representing the true spirit of Wisdom-"Sophia" in the Greek, residing within Freemasonry, as within all Ancient Initiatory Mystery Traditions.

As we explored in earlier chapters, the secret war on human consciousness uses the technique of usurpation, substitution, even mimicry, to captivate and enchant the masses into buying into the narrowed and specialized scope of reality, a vicious cycle that is progressive and self-perpetuating, effectively limiting the field of possibilities and potential. When an abridged version of knowledge and wisdom is readily accepted wholesale, holding back the tide would be easier than changing mass perception.

However, for those individual Masons on a quest for truth and understanding, higher knowledge and wisdom, this will not do. And though the path is not easy, and the way forward narrow and fraught with difficulties, the aspiring adept is *choosing* the Hermetic path; he is consciously enlisting to struggle, and though often it seems against the very fabric of our realities, our consciousness and spiritual development, like most *real* growth, it is at times painful, gradual, and often imperceptible, but in the end far more meaningful and rewarding.

And so, the demographic of Freemasonry continues to divide into sub-groups of belief and approach. There are those who subscribe to the Antient, or Ancient, approach embodied in the York Rite of American Ancient Craft Masonry, and there are adherents to the European "Continental" more Modern modification of the Scottish Rite traditions. A man could join to fulfill a timeless quest for divine truth, or to simply achieve social or political status and or business success. Some subscribe to the notion that Freemasonry is only the three degrees of the Blue Lodge, while others think the Higher Degrees are important, even necessary, to true Masonic Education. Some are of the perception that the timeless mysteries are encoded within the esoteric teachings, while there are those who see nothing at all to the secrets and symbolic instruction therein, aside from the obvious virtue and moral teachings presented.

What we are left with as the end result, an effect felt within the greater fraternity, is that membership in the August halls of Freemasonry on the whole is in a general state of decline, as is the case with many voluntary organizations in America in the 21st century. The distinction within freemasonry remains clear to this writer, as someone who has sat in the sidelines of regular lodge communications, as well as being invited into the exclusive lodges of research to discuss the far more esoteric sides of tradition; there is a serious lack of education and understanding within the fraternity. It is possible that for those seeking the "Lazy Man's" path to enlightenment, or for the sake of material benefit, this does not matter. Lazy Man could simply pay a high fee, show up for an evening class or weekend seminar, and observe glorified, overindulged pageants and mock-ceremonies, in order to receive a fancy certificate awarding him the status of a 32nd degree "Sublime Prince of the Royal Secret" or the like.

The secret, it turns out, being how very meaningless and contrived the entire rite really is! If "lucky", one might receive the equally meaningless, yet far more potentially damaging, "honorary" (which means you did nothing to actually earn the degree-besides pay the fee) 33rd Degree and may even be elected Sovereign Grand Inspector General and an active member of the Supreme Council, by secret ballot and unanimous vote of Active Members present. Membership in the Supreme Council carries the implication (left over from the Continental System and reinforced in America) that they "inspect" the other Masons in Masonry through the Supreme Council's self-declared mission to root out other "spurious" irregular orders, degrees, and rites-it takes one to know one I guess.

Thus, armed with your newly issued plastic pyramid with faux-gold ring encased inside bearing the Hebrew insignia co-opted by the order, snappy bell-hop cap complete with leather pill-box case, and of course your fancy certificate you can go forth-as a recognized authority, free to mislead and misinform others and otherwise divert Freemasonry from its true purpose, as you see fit.

And that's exactly what has happened for generations. The average post-modern Freemason (especially American) has neither the time, nor inclination, to submit to the kind of struggle which is required for real inner growth; a goal which offers far greater metaphysical rewards than a fancy patent with gold seal one can get with no true inner growth or struggle at all. And the system remains counterfeited, degraded by and with this condition.

Quite obviously, all those involved have a vested interest in maintaining the hoax, if for no greater reason than, were the truth known, those falsely entitled "adepts", "princes", or "masters" would be exposed as frauds, along with their farcical system. Therein lies the rub; the hitch which keeps the status quo in place, maintaining the illusory paradigm. Fear of exposure is a powerful motivator.

So, is it really possible? Is this the biggest secret revealed? Is there truly no substance to the rituals and elaborate teachings of the system, nor the fancifully fabricated histories and traditions of one of the world's largest, wealthiest, and most powerful quasi-Masonic fraternal lodge traditions? Could the entire Scottish Rite system be based on a series of novelty, exhibition, and side-degrees; never presented as, or intended to be, anything more than the endeavor of a self-important modified innovation?

Is there nothing else to all this? Is there nothing more to consider, nothing else to give pause, with regards to a master plan, a blueprint for tyranny and control? Is it possible that behind all the philosophical expositions and pseudo-spiritual musings, beyond the base "way of equilibrium", which is almost exclusively focused within the approach presented in Morals and Dogma (even though said equilibrium is commenced and achieved within the Blue Lodge degrees), there is a more sinister design for humanity?

Did the early architects of the Ancient and Accepted Rite, many of whom were powerful leaders of the Confederacy *and* the Federal Government of America, harness the esoteric system and hierarchical structure afforded and inherent within fraternal lodge systems such as the Scottish Rite (which harbored the so-called Ineffable Degrees), for their own plan to conquer human societies and subjugate the world to the vision of a global, race-based, "slavocracy"?

We will consider these questions and more in pages that follow.

8

SCOTTISH RITE SYSTEM OF CONTROL

As one might expect, things took a drastic turn when I made it known to the Scottish Rite status quo within my home Lodge that I would not in fact be petitioning the Scottish Rite Valley for membership in their order.

Where there had once been the warmth of brotherly love and friendship, there was now a cold void of disdain. Suddenly all support by brothers once enthusiastic to help with proposed activities and events was retracted to the bare minimal, seemingly present only to witness the failure of endeavors. Dinners and public functions, for which I volunteered to cook and organize, designed to inspired growth of membership in the Blue Lodge, would be sparsely attended. I was left to plan and prepare, cook, and serve a full dinner for over 30 people with minimal help from the same brothers in the SR who, prior to my choice *not* to join the Scottish Rite, had pledged support but were now seemingly unavailable to help.

One 33rd degree white cap, who had previously made a point of telling my wife I was "a genius" and with whom nary a bad word had passed between us, was now openly slandering my name; declaring in front of more than one brother, "I hate that guy!" and telling other brothers I owed the Blue Lodge money, even though the supposed "loan" was from the said Scottish Rite's Almoners Fund, a charitable organization which I came to find out does not *loan* money, and is in point of fact, completely separate from the Blue Lodge!

At every meeting I went to, there was an agent from the Scottish Rite, giving me knowing glances. Some, like the two brothers who had given me the money directly, would confront me every time they saw me, reminding me I needed to pay back the money "as soon as humanly possible." It was terribly degrading, and demoralizing. I continued to make payments when I could, though I was still unable to find full time employment. It amounted to me having my pockets picked every time I went to a lodge meeting.

After a year in the Blue Lodge, I petitioned the York Rite to complete my Ancient Craft Masonry education and receive further light in Freemasonry. Judgment was palpable from this decision and sealed my fate to be marginalized and weakened politically beyond repair in my home lodge. These brothers thought I should pay back the money before I progressed through the other degrees. Once you upset the status quo apple cart there's no getting back on-not in the lifetime of those key members driving the cart anyway.

Any marginalizing they might have done to me was made moot however, when, shortly after joining the York Rite I transferred my membership to a lodge one city over, the home lodge of the Grand York Rite Secretary who had helped initiate me into the York Rite. He was fast becoming a friend and mentor in Masonry, as well as Brother and "Companion" as we referred to each other in the York Rite. The Secretary "Recorder" of the local York Rite organization in the city of my residence also took special interest and time to mentor me, for which I will ever be grateful.

These men and others like them are the "way-showers" for sincere seekers, who always appear to guide us on our journey of discovery. When I explained the situation with the Almoners Fund to him and other mentors in the York Rite, I was assured I did not in fact owe any money-being former members of the SR themselves they knew the rules and regulations. The Almoner's Fund was not for loaning money. All monies given were gifts of the fund. The brothers who had "loaned" me the money under duress had been totally out of line, and out of order.

To speak now of the experience of being initiated into the American York Rite system the complete system of American Ancient Craft Masonry seems somewhat surreal to recall. It remains beyond words to truly describe the initiatory process contained within such esoteric systems as the Western Fraternal Lodges in general but especially the series of degrees which completes the Candidate's (or pilgrim's) journey. This has always been the point though, and this is how it was for me as well. Real secrets are beyond risk of exposure as they can only truly be conveyed through experience.

Though "life", with all its tests and travails (as always then and now), may have insinuated itself into the moment serving to detract or divert a portion of awareness (as it always does) away from the greater experience at hand. This did not serve to diminish the experience one iota. Now many of the voices, who delivered the ritual of the York Rite to me, have long since been silenced by the common and universal mortality that will one day quiet us all; they live and speak on in the august halls of my most cherished memories and recollections.

Not long after I was "dubbed" a Knight Templar, the pinnacle of the degree progression within Ancient Craft degrees in America, I was invited to join several side orders. These various orders were actually custodians of several groups of antiquated degrees left over from the 18th-19th century degree-making frenzy. The Knight Mason Degrees (or "Irish Degrees"), which contained the oldest rituals still in continuous practice: the Knight of Sword, Knight of the East, and Knight of the East and West, represented the "working class" chivalric orders from the Continental Degree Systems. The "Scotch" Masons, deriving their myth and tradition from the crusades when all knights of holy orders were nobility this being a prerequisite, served as representative of the "noble class".

A rift formed within the lodge with these "Scotch-ish" Masons assuming a higher rank by distinction of social class, indirectly through the orders of chivalry, which often led to leadership positions within the structure of Freemasonry. Just the sort of divisive "traditional" observance we find in Blue Lodges today! The average working class Mason wished to match the distinction and honor of membership in an order of chivalry, but one that qualifies to his rank and station, and so the Knight of the Sword degree was born.

I was also invited to join the Allied Masonic Degree Order (AMD), which possessed over a dozen degrees from the Continental System, many of them very similar to ones contained within the Rite of Perfection system; the Royal Ark Mariner, Order of the Secret Monitor, Knight of Constantinople, and the Grand Architect; all understandably resembling various degrees within the York Rite and Scottish Rite, in that most of the degrees found their genesis in the same Continental System. The most exciting invitation I received, and the one I sought most, was membership in the Masonic College of Rosicrucians (SRICF). I actually flew back to the Midwest from Massachusetts to be initiated into this Order.

I would also fly to Washington DC a few years later to be initiated into the third and highest order within the SRICF, the High Council being made an 8th Grade Magister Templi (Master of the Temple) the second highest degree in this particular order and subordinate only to the 9th Grade Chief Adept. As a member of the High Order, I was eligible to be appointed to the Secretary's Chair of the College, which I was so appointed by the Supreme Magus of the High Council in DC. The third Order within the SRICF, contains the two degrees (8th-9th Grades) mentioned above.

These invitations and appointments were a direct result of my associations with key members of the York Rite in my local area who were active in leadership roles in various side orders, and recognized my potential for research and presentation, as well as being an asset to the York Rite.

Over the course of my Masonic career I wrote and presented several papers in each order I belonged to. They were usually coolly received, given the most minimal response on all occasions. I explored a wide variety of subjects surrounding Freemasonry proper, and grew to understand the universal teachings encoded within the whole system.

I was even further insulated from any repercussions, from the Scottish Rite, for joining the York Rite by the decision in 2009 to uproot our family once again and move some 2000 miles away, back to the Northeast, to return to the family business and the land of my birth. My people being from a very "affluent" region of New England, allowing even "servant-class", entry-level wage slaves such as my wife and I to eke out a comparable existence to anywhere else, and even though the "non-affluent" lived lives of constant struggle, when you add the surrounding beauty of a colonial fishing village scenery, it's an attractive prospect.

In my newly self-imposed exile from my home lodge, I was left to study and research the "further light" in Masonry on my own. I literally consumed every book, paper, and lecture I could find on the subjects surrounding, and contained within Freemasonry. I did, however, yearn for fellowship and a chance to review the rituals I had advanced thru-but from the "side-line" as a spectator for comparative research and experience. I had the unique opportunity to affiliate myself with the Lodge system of my home town and surrounding jurisdiction.

Eventually I would go forth seeking fellowship once again, only to be confronted by the Scottish Rite and its agents, this time on the Northern Jurisdiction Supreme Council's turf. This jurisdiction mirroring the same program as the Southern though even more overtly class-oriented than in the Mid-West, right down to the complete absence of Masonic Education, even from the Stated Communication agenda in the new jurisdiction I moved to!!

Many differences can be found between the Northern and Southern jurisdictions. The Northern Jurisdiction Supreme Council governs the Scottish Rite located in the original 13 colony states of America; the Southern governs the remaining 37 states in the Union. In the system of my home lodge in the Midwest, as with all the others in the domain, Masonic Education was usually one of the last things covered in a normal Stated Communication business meeting, which are held monthly in many

Blue Lodges year-round. It was shocking to find Masonic Education was not even on the list of priorities in the Lodges on the East coast, where Freemasonry was transplanted from Europe and first spread in America. What a clear commentary on the effects, the results of emphasis on accolades and honors, title and prestige over real substance, true enlightenment gained through study in the actual pursuit of knowledge and sacred wisdom.

Here, once again, the substitution of one teaching and approach for another still under the guise of the former was evident. A counterfeit reality, limiting education and veiling the truth, sows discord and brings forth chaos and stagnation and haunting uncertainty.

There were slight variations to the ritual in both Blue Lodge jurisdictions I was then affiliated with, but the core teachings and ideals remained intact. I was very impressed with the proficiency of the New England brethren. And the formality seemed somehow fitting. All officers, in subordinate lodges as well as the Grand Lodge, wore formal tuxedos and gloves at all times, and for every official "stated communication" (monthly general business meetings), or special degree work . It is most satisfying to witness the rituals when delivered with such grace and proficiency.

There was a particular Canadian Charge that was employed during the 3rd degree at the close of the work, that was fascinating, and I set about memorizing the part myself, not only to deliver to the brethren back in the Midwest as an exhibition for Masonic Education, but also to be available to do the work in my new jurisdiction in the New England Lodges. It had been my experience that the majority of American Freemasons don't bother to learn a part in the Ritual-much less assume a role or part in actual degree work-due to the fact that all parts were voluntary, resulting in a constant need for Brothers willing to learn the various parts. In witnessing such proficiency and zeal, I therefore believed my enthusiasm would be welcomed, but as I would eventually discover, this was quite to the contrary. And it was here where the trouble began for me in my new Lodge.

Each Lodge must fill the parts of the principle officers/players in the Ritual in order to conduct degree work in any given Lodge; as a voluntary organization and with the present decline in active members in such organizations, this often proves more difficult to imagine than one might expect. Often times, a Lodge is compelled to solicit "courtesy work" from members of neighboring Lodges in the same district or jurisdiction. With this tradition, an individual brother proficient in degree work may end up affiliated to several lodges in a given district or surrounding jurisdiction. As such, any particularly proficient brother may find himself in a sort of quasi-celebrity status as a visiting mercenary, or "hired-gun", for degree work, and if such individuals learned to recite the ritual with any sort of flair or dramatics, all the better for his prestige among his peers.

There was one such individual, among a handful with comparable proficiency, in the new jurisdiction I had moved to. He was an excellent ritualist, without equal in the district. He was also an active member of the Scottish Rite, who when I met him, was finally branching out into the York Rite and other concordant orders. He was extremely ambitious, and had personally mastered the Canadian Charge in the 3rd degree, among many other parts in the rituals of all three degrees.

This Brother, whom we will call "Brother A", was the Master of a very prestigious Lodge, in an exclusive art community, that had a retail space on the street level below, which saw yearly profits of over $80,000, due to a high volume tourists trade. At first, Brother A was friendly and accommodating, and seemed generally interested in what I had to share with regards to the York Rite and Ancient Craft Masonry in America.

The Lodge had a long history, having been chartered by none other than Paul Revere during his three years as Grand Master in the late 1700's; he chartered more lodges than any other GM in Massachusetts Masonic history. Contained within Brother A's Lodge was a complete set of working tools of the craft, handmade in pure silver by Sir Knight Brother Revere himself.

The gavel used by the Master of the Lodge was one of a set of three which were carved from the mainsail mast of a decommissioned Continental Navy Battleship that fought in the Revolution against Great Britain. The gavel was presented to the Lodge in 1902 by then New York Governor Teddy Roosevelt, also a Master Mason.

In this new district, which was literally the birthplace of the American Rite (Thomas Webb's home Commandery being the Grand Commandery of Massachusetts and Rhode Island) I found that the York Rite was in an even worse state than the Midwest! Besides the Blue Lodge, the local traditions in Massachusetts kept the three orders within the York Rite-the Chapter, Council, and Commandery-separate and autonomous, thus slowing the Candidate's progress through the orders within the Rite to the point where Brother Companions were not entering all the orders nor completing all the degrees. Their masonic education being left unfinished, many of these brothers would lose interest in the York Rite, having incomplete views of the whole system experientially as well as intellectually.

Brother A was anxious to progress through all the degrees of the York Rite and be dubbed a Knight Templar, most probably to legitimize any claims to such status as an active member of the Scottish Rite-which would have the world believe it is the only rightful heir to "Templar Masonry". As I began to share my findings and understanding with the brethren, I realized Brother A possessed little or no real knowledge of the esoteric and symbolic aspects to Freemasonry that I had gathered and concluded from my own research and experiences. He was out of his element and he knew it. I found a group of new comers to the Craft forming around me before each meeting to hear my Masonic perspectives. There was serious talk of forming a study club.

To make matters even worse, seeing the urgent need for some kind of educational presence in the local lodge system, I concluded my mandate was to establish a Lodge of Research, which I had been yearning to form in the Midwest District and would have had I not moved. Everyone I queried was eager to join such a body and begged to be kept posted as to the progress of such a project. It seemed like destiny to me.

What I did not know, was that Brother A was already involved in a Grand Lodge project to revise and endorse a new state-wide Lodge of Research, approved and controlled exclusively by the Grand Lodge, which would serve all the districts in the State and present a uniform and official version of Masonic Research to all Masons. This would be a research lodge of a whole different breed; not at all like the locally formed and administered research body I had imagined, which would naturally grow in the district serving the specific needs of each area Lodge and its members. There could, and should, be a lodge of research in every subordinate Lodge to offer an educational forum for members craving more light than was provided in general.

All this came to head on the long, lonely drive home, with myself and Brother A, the night he was initiated into the Cryptic Council and made a Royal and Select Master, in a neighboring lodge. As often happens, the York Rite Companions would all gather in a centrally-located Masonic center to do courtesy degree work in any given making new York Rite Masons.

I played the part of conducting the Candidates through the ritual. I led the prospective new members to the Council from one part of the ceremony to the next answering all questions with the required responses. Having been already made Royal Arch Masons (this being the prerequisite to be initiated into the Royal and Select Master degrees and joining the Cryptic Council), the Companion Candidates-of which there were two that night-were, by this time, already familiar with at least 7 degrees in Ancient Craft Masonry. I had prepared a small talk, drawn from Mackey's Masonic Ritualist (a pocket-book from 1867, which I found in one of the many used bookstores I haunted), that expounded on the symbolism of the degrees they had just witnessed and had been guided through. The night went over without a hitch and both Candidates were very pleased and impressed with what they had experienced.

On the ride home, Brother A and I spoke more on Masonry and the various rituals and orders therein. At some point he made it very clear that he did not appreciate me trying to "usurp" his "favorite part" of the 3rd degree, the Canadian Charge! He also made it clear that I would never deliver that charge if he was in Lodge, not even in my new "home lodge", at least 45 minutes away from where he lived. This was, unfortunately, not the only thing he made clear to me that night. When I mentioned my plan to launch a local Lodge of Research body in my home lodge he scoffed that it would "never happen".

"The Grand Lodge will never approve such autonomy," he said, cynically. When I mentioned that many of the brothers in his own Lodge had expressed interest in joining my proposed Lodge of Research (including his own Secretary!), he declared that all the brethren would "do as they were told!" He then informed me of the project already underway, which would be unveiled "in a very short time" and launched throughout the state. He was very condescending and outright offensive.

Needless to say, I was very demoralized after that talk. I felt frustrated and hopeless. And I noticed right away a "cooling off" where there had once been a frenzy of interest in the things I was discovering and reviewing before; now no one answered when I called or responded to my emails. The small group, that began to gather before and after Lodge, was no more, it just seemed to fade away.

I became indignant and went to the Secretary Recorder of the local York Rite Bodies, a counterpart of my mentor back in the Midwest one of the Guardians of the "Grail-truths" about Ancient Craft Masonry. I met with this Companion, who also happened to be a high-ranking local Grand Representative of the Grand York Rite Offices, to discuss this fellow

Companion's conduct and seek his advice as to my wisest course of action.

That meeting, in an empty Lodge space in the time between Dinner and the commencement of the Stated Communication, will forever be imprinted in my mind as the moment when I realized that any idea I had of a "Masonic Career" was impossible. This Brother was appropriately embittered and cynical; having had 30+ years' active membership in one of the snobbiest, most judgmental, and "classist" Lodge Systems in America. Upon hearing my complaints, he made himself loud and clear to me when he interrupted me and demanded gruffly that I take a seat in the sidelines, as he paced back and forth before me.

"Look guy," he said shaking his head, "you need to understand how things work around here. You can't come in here with all your big ideas and questions and speculations. You are upsetting the apple-cart (where I got the term) here! There are brothers in these Lodges who think, and want everyone else to think, they are the smartest guys in the room. You are upsetting that whole status quo. And now let me tell you something and I hope you hear this, if you continue on your present course, these same individuals will target you, and they WILL destroy you! Believe it, because I have seen it happen before!"

Just like that. The shells fell away from my eyes for good. I knew the game was over. I went home and resolved to never return to the Lodges, in Massachusetts at the very least, again. I was utterly disturbed by the experience. For several months following this exchange, I completely withdrew any and all associations with the Lodge or Masons in my hometown, and would have probably have never looked back had I not received a series of calls out of the blue, about 6 months after that incident, from three of the several Brother Companions I had grown close to before all the trouble began in Massachusetts. Each of these three brothers contacted me separately regarding the formation of another Research body in the local district!

What they were proposing was the formation of an Allied Masonic Degrees (AMD) Council in our area which, as I mentioned above, is by design a research Lodge stewarding their own set of degrees and offering a forum for peer review of research papers, etc. What these brothers lacked was an active Knight of Constantinople (the initiating degree of the order) to co-sign the charter application, the other 6 signers of the application having to be Royal Arch Masons in good standing.

As a Knight of Constantinople, and active member of my home

council of AMD in the Midwest, I was qualified to meet the requirements. The three Companions who had chosen to reach out to me were all good men who meant well. They were carefully picked to be most persuasive, appealing not only to my ego and desire to form a research body already, but also to the sentimentality which seemed to influence me with regards to freemasonry in such a short time. And it worked. I agreed to help them form the Council. Then came the hitch…

I was informed that my favorite Brother A, the ritualist who had single-handedly driven me out of the Massachusetts Lodge system, would *"have to"* be a part of this Council in order to secure "the proper prestige and validity among the more discerning brethren"; as a matter of fact he would be made the very first presiding officer, listed on the official charter as the Sovereign Master.

I was offered the Secretary Chair, a position I took because of the control I knew I would have in order to maintain its stated purpose as a research lodge and, as explicitly stated within the bylaws, I would maintain possession of the physical charter that I and the six other Royal Arch Masons would sign. I even made arrangements with a local bank knowing the vice president to be a brother Blue Lodge Mason to purchase a safe deposit box in order to properly store the charter and council archives.

It was all a sham. As soon as the Council application was approved, and the date set to "constitute" the Council, everything changed. First, Brother A called a secret meeting without me, the acting secretary, and "laid down the law". He made it clear, to all present, the Council was *his* to run, and how he intended to run it was to offer memberships to "influential and successful" masons of his choosing. That Council membership would be dangled like a carrot to said Brothers, to form and elite "supper club" where they would all dress in tuxedos and preen about, back-slapping each other and acting important and prestigious. I was informed of this by one of the other Companions who had signed the Charter Application as well, but was horrified by this sudden sea change of intent. I was disgusted, aghast, and enraged. I had been suckered, played like a fiddle, and I wanted satisfaction.

I emailed the Secretary General of the AMD Grand Council, who was also the Secretary General of the Knight Masons Grand Council and the High Council of the SRICF (American Rosicrucians). I laid it all out and informed him of everything that transpired, as recounted above, honestly and completely. I requested, specifically, that the charter application be denied and cancelled immediately. I even attached an account from the Companion who had been present at the Secret meeting and reported the goings-on to me! I sat back and waited for the response and probable blowback I expected. I heard nothing.

I waited a few more days and re-sent the email, with a query if the message was being received. Still I heard nothing. I tried phoning the Secretary directly at his home outside Washington, DC, and left two voice mails. He never called me back. I might point out that I had dealt with the Secretary General already thru email, phone and mail, ordering various research materials from him for the Orders we belonged to, he as Secretary General, and having already established such a rapport, I believed that he would respond.

After a week of anxiety over the situation, I managed to get him on the phone. To my great surprise and befuddlement, he casually affirmed that he received all of my messages and attempts at contact! When I asked him why he had not contacted me, he sighed and said, "Now look... I spoke with Brother A (whom he called by first name!). He and I, both, agree that you are getting a bit over excited here. I mean, I don't know what you expect to happen here, but I will not by cancelling the charter, that's for sure!" I couldn't believe my ears! When I asked him directly why he had called Brother A, yet not contacted me at all, he evasively sidestepped the question and said, "OK, I get it, you don't like Brother A. Well now, do you realize that you hold Absolute Power over that Council?" I didn't know what to say. "What do you mean?" I asked, very apprehensive.

"Well now, don't quote me on this-and I will deny it if you do-but, if you want to get rid of someone in the Council, it's easy."

"I-I don't follow you. How can I *do* that?" I stammered more freaked out than ever. He made a sound like a quiet snicker or chuckle and in a very knowing tone he said,

"It's very simple really. If you want somebody gone, just 'neglect' to send them a dues notice and when they don't pay dues, well, you can suspend them for 'non-payment of dues', of course! They will get the message." It was as simple as that, right? No. No, this was wrong, very wrong! Imagine if you will the evil emperor from Star Wars when we takes over the Republic and cries out "Ab-sol-ute pow-er!!!" It was SO creepy and unsettling, needless to say, that was the final straw. Very soon after that I demitted from the Lodges I had affiliated with in New England; which means I deactivated my membership, something only a Freemason in good standing, as in all dues paid, can do. I deleted every Mason's phone number from my phone and blocked all the emails from all Massachusetts Freemasons. No one from any lodge ever called or came by my house again. It was like it never happened.

By this time I had already begun broadcasting first on The Free Zone and then Radio Free Humanity on AFR Network-the first incarnation of my weekly internet radio show, later changed to The Middle Chamber - which I now co-host w/ my wife Mater X at middlechambermedia.com. It seemed a perfect way for me to transition away from active membership in the "Lodge", while still utilizing the knowledge and insights I had acquired about esoteric orders. It seems MANY people worldwide are now very interested in Fraternal Orders such as the Freemasons, Knights Templar, and Rosicrucians, among so many more.

Soon after that the economy in my home town finally started feeling the effects of the Great Recession of the 21st century in America. The family business lost about 40% of their clientele, and they were not replaced; prompting a bit of reorganization and downsizing to meet the changes in the market. There was a new face on the wealthy moving to coastal New England, and they didn't care about spending as much money on personal gardeners, and caretakers for their vacation homes and estates.

After 3 1/2 years paying upwards of $60,000 in rent alone, not to mention the high cost of living in a beautiful area, moving our family of six 5 times from one winter rental/summer rental/yearly rental to another in the same area, we opted to return to the Midwest and give it another try in the little college town city we still call home to this day. When I returned to my "Mother Lodge" in the Midwest, I tried to return to active membership with the brethren there, especially the remaining mentors, the "guardians of the grail" from my early membership, these brothers endangered now, as many have passed on to the "Celestial Lodge" above, taking their rightful place in the line of the Brotherhood of the Mystic Tie in Eternity.

It's hard to watch the decline of those that remain. The metaphor is not lost on me; they reflect the condition of Freemasonry as a whole. I realized once again with a heavy heart, that Freemasonry was all done for me, as far as active membership goes anyways. It was impossible to fight the tide overtaking the leadership of the Grand Lodges, as well as all the subordinate ones. It was all too clear that, aside from the occasional rarity, most lodges are content with the direction of the fraternity as a whole-no matter the reality, or substance, of teachings and principles, nor the motivation of the leadership.

And, it really is no fun fighting a revolution all by yourself...

9

BANKSTER THUGS AND WHITE CAPS

"It is far easier to fool a man than it is to convince him he is being fooled." ~Mark Twain

But the question still remains, even at this late hour here, in these pages. Have we answered it? Have we clearly reviewed the facts and events leading to our present day condition? How can any Supreme Council, in the entire history and tradition of the Rite of Perfection/Scottish Rite, insist on its primacy and exert its authority over any other Supreme Council from anything resembling a legitimate stance? In a roomful of frauds and make believe who truly rules and reigns supreme? It seems much more like a case of "in the land of the blind the one-eyed man is king…"

Let us consider further, before we conclude, the term "degree"; as we have mentioned it throughout this work. We should clarify more just *what* one means. Henry Coil defines it as meaning "…some esoteric ceremony, no matter how brief, which advances the member or candidate to a 'higher' rank including the communication to him of particular distinguishing words, signs, grips, tokens, or other esoteric matter, those of each degree being denied to members of lower degrees as firmly as they are denied to complete strangers…" [58]

The book, Lodge of the Double-Headed Eagle: Two Centuries of Scottish Rite Freemasonry in America's Southern Jurisdiction, written by William Fox in 1997, reports there were actually 11,000 such degrees in the Continental systems, and that it was from these various degree systems the Rite of Perfection was born and carried to the "New World". And, as we have already considered, Stephen (Etienne) Morin went forth to propagate the 25 degrees of the Rite, operating under the empowerment of a questionable body (or bodies) in France, in San Domingo after being captured at sea by the British, taken to London and finally released due to his acquaintance with a Count Ferrers (the then current Grand Master of the Grand Lodge of England.)

Looking at Morin's empowerment closely, tracing it back to the commonly proposed genesis point of the Rite of Perfection and inevitably the Scottish Rite, we find the early Councils such as those in Paris, which evolved into the bodies which established the Grand Constitutions of 1786, and before that, the Constitutions of 1782. Tracing back from present day in an imaginary unbroken line, we could establish a core root of the organizations recognized by the Supreme Council(s) today. So it is worth it, at this time, to look at a few parts of these Constitutions from late 18th century European Freemasonry.

According to William Fox, several Articles within the Constitutions are worthy of note. For example, Article 3 makes allotments for the higher degrees of 30th through 33rd, which obviously became permanent; also an allotment to remit payments to the Grand Commander, General Secretary, and Supreme Council. These Constitutions laid the groundwork for the hierarchical structure and authority of the Supreme Council(s), and eventually many lodges across America and the globe. Article V establishes the remarkable prerequisite that 4 out of 9 active members, of any given Supreme Council, must profess belief in the prevailing religious belief of a given nation state; at least as Albert Pike interpreted it, because he was given final word on the subject with his professional legal assessment of the Article viewed as official.

There was a dissenting view for the record: Frederick Dalcho, 1st Lt. Grand Commander of the Knights Templar of South Carolina, claimed long before Pike that the text of *his* English version of the Constitutions stated the prerequisite called for 5 of the 9 active members, showing Pike's assessment to be a contradiction. In Article VIII of the 1786 Constitutions, adopted by both French and German Freemasonry, a provision was set for the formation of a Grand Consistory; this is the earliest reference to a Grand Consistory in association with the Rite of Perfection.

Taking these examples from the "Lodge of the Double Headed Eagle", it should be noted that the author, all but directly, implied the body being governed at the time of the Constitutions was the Scottish Rite, which we conclude from all previous research and review to be a stretch of the imagination at best, and a deliberate mistruth at worst.

To note the Article mentioned calls for a Grand Consistory to be composed of "Prince Masons of the Royal Secret of the 32nd degree" whose acts were to have no force "without the previous sanction of the Supreme Council of the 33rd degree"; in other words, there may *appear* to be a democratic system, but in reality nothing would be done without the preapproval of the Supreme Council, in all affairs! A complete totalitarian government, not unlike the Vatican Papal structure with the College of

Cardinals.

The governing body in America, a.k.a the Mother Council of the world, was first opened, in 1801, in South Carolina by Frederick Dalcho and Colonel John Mitchell, both Sovereign Grand Inspector Generals, three months after Thomas Jefferson was elected our third president. Jefferson's campaign was steeped in anti-masonic and anti-illuminati rhetoric and accusations; not surprising, in that foreign bankster-thugs, who might also be referred to as Agents of the Illuminati or Agents of social chaos, had infiltrated the newly forming American government even before the Revolution was over.

In fact, the First Central Bank of America-organized by Alexander Hamilton, suspected agent of the European/Rothschild bankster-thugs-was already chartered before the Treaty of Paris, which ended overt hostilities between England and America, was signed. This charter was not renewed by Congress when it ran out due to the massive failure, on the part of the Bank, to do anything but cause financial ruin in its wake. There would be several "attempts" to establish a new Central Bank, until the system of wealth extraction was realized and perfected with the Federal Reserve System.

When that first Supreme Council met, they were obviously still referring to their fledgling system as the Ineffable Degrees. As we have discovered, it is highly probable that at no time before 1860 did the Ineffable Degrees, soon-to-be called the Scottish Rite Southern Jurisdiction, exceed 500 members in the entire world; in 1880 the first statistical report reads 1150 members total. By 1890, one year before Albert Pike's death, there were under 3,000 members who belonged to the Scottish Rite, worldwide.

In 1802, when the Supreme Council met in South Carolina, there was a slave rebellion in Haiti; a French jeweler, named Joseph Cerneau, fled to Cuba for safety, only to be expelled from there in 1806. Cerneau was one of several key individuals who latched onto the Rite of Perfection and rode it to the next level of their journey in "Freemasonry", and in life it seems. Having first emigrated from France to San Domingo in the 1780's, Cerneau was involved in Masonic Activities on both sides of the Atlantic. He seems to have been empowered, in a limited capacity, as a Deputy Inspector General in the Rite of Perfection, to confer the first 24 degrees of the Rite, and was permitted to offer the 25th degree to one candidate a year-but not outside Cuba!

As many men who come into contact with this system seem to do,

Cerneau decided he was entitled (though it is uncertain how) to all the degrees he discovered available to the Rite of Perfection. In November 1806, Joseph Cerneau reached New York, where he promptly ignored the clearly explicit limitations of his patent. After establishing a Grand and Sovereign Grand Consistory of the USA, without any clear authority, Cerneau formed his most spurious body of all, a Supreme Council in New York; which apparently never met.

It seems Cerneau operated what was then referred to as a "diploma mill", and he did not confine himself to the Ineffable Degrees; with the York Rite quite obviously more prosperous than the Rite of Perfection, Cerneau established a Grand Encampment of NY, in 1814, to empower himself to confer the Knight Templar degree. This was completely out of order with all Templar Masonry in America; not that this was a rare or unusual occurrence. From the birth of Freemasonry in America, to the present, we find the field of esoteric fraternal orders is peppered with "clandestine", or "spurious", Freemasonry and its Concordant Orders. Cerneau, himself, had never even been formally initiated into the Masonic Order of the Temple and therefore was not a Knight Templar!

Cerneau had friends in high places, enlisting the aid of a very influential New York Mason, Dewitt Clinton-then Mayor of New York City-to legitimize his claims; once again, wealth and influence allowing for great errors to be committed in the name of Freemasonry. Clinton was Governor of New York State, first from 1817-1822 and again from 1825-1828, during the infamous "Morgan Affair" in 1826, and was largely responsible for the historic opening of the Eerie Canal in 1825. He was also bitter rivals with Daniel Tompkins, who served as governor 1807-1817 and also as the 6th Vice President of the United States, who was the first Grand Commander of the Northern Jurisdiction of the Scottish Rite from 1813-1825.

When Cerneau returned to France in 1827, he left several subordinate bodies of his version of the Rite established in Louisiana, Massachusetts, Pennsylvania, and South Carolina, as well as Brazil, Colombia, Puerto Rico, and Venezuela; though most of these expired during the Anti-Masonic fervor which took place between the years 1832-1840. Only his Rite of Perfection Bodies in New Orleans and Charleston survived that period of time. "Cerneauism" would be a thorn in the side of the Rite, and Grand Commander Pike, for many years to come.

In 1824, the Supreme Council of South Carolina issued letters-patent for the establishment of a Supreme Council of 33rd for Ireland, the first instance of a Supreme Council being established, directly by letters patent from the Mother Council of the World. The next year, the famous Marquis de Lafayette, the beloved French Officer of the American Revolution and also a distinguished Mason, visited Charleston during his celebrated tour of the U.S.

The Charleston Courier reported the Supreme Council had originally intended to meet and confer an Honorary 33rd Degree upon the Marquis, furthering the proscribed practice Pike would also endorse to legitimize and lend authenticity and authority to the Rite by recruiting the famous and influential brethren of Freemasonry, along with all the appendant degrees of the Rite of Perfection. In fact, the Supreme Council did not convene, "…finding the Marquis stay would be too short to admit him".

A possible factor being that "the Cerneau group in New York had (already) conferred the 33rd upon Lafayette…much to the disgust of the Supreme Council in Charleston." [68] The Marquis subsequently met with no bodies of the Ancient and Accepted Rite, choosing instead to confine his reception to the Knights Templar Commandery only!

According Lodge of the Double-Headed Eagle, "Captain" William claimed to have served as Captain during the War of 1812, and while several listings for the name 'William Morgan' from his birthplace in Virginia, none with the rank of Captain are found. One can also see the works of Stephen Defoe, for more insight on the subject.

What is apparently the case here, Morgan faked being a Blue Lodge Master Mason in order to be initiated into the Royal Arch and the Knights Templar Degrees. Morgan was rumored to be a low bottom gambler and alcoholic, prone to running up debts and cavorting about the village, inebriated and in full Templar regalia, much to the chagrin and dismay of local Masonic brethren. When he was revealed as a fraud, his name was removed from the charter of a newly formed local Royal Arch Chapter that he helped establish. It was then he made threats and preparations to publish his expose.

Legend has it, on the 11th of September, 1825, after having been remanded on possible trumped-up charges of debt; Morgan was released from the jail in Canandaigua, NY, into the recognizance of several men, known to be local Masons. He was then spirited away in the back of a wagon, never to be seen or heard from again, in America; supposedly abducted because he was about to publish an expose of the Freemasonic Rituals entitled, *Illustrations of Masonry: By One of the Fraternity Who*

Has Devoted 30 Years to the Subject. Many Masons claim he was taken to Canada and paid a pension never to return. Others say that he was thrown over the falls at Niagara in a rum barrel; a badly decomposed body was found in the Niagara River a short time after his disappearance had been identified as him. Although Morgan's abduction was ultimately proved in court, his murder was not, and remains a mystery to this day.

The introduction to another famous American Masonic expose, Richardson's Monitor matter-of-factly states that Masons killed "Captain" William Morgan.

The news of "The Morgan Affair" generated a pronounced reaction against Masonry, not only in New York, but all over America. The trial of those charged covered a period of 5 years and helped to keep the Anti-Masonic cauldron boiling. Some twenty Grand Juries were called; 54 Masons were indicted, 39 brought to trial, and 10 received convictions and jail terms ranging from 30 days to 28 months. Of the 10 Masons who were convicted, six actually participated in Morgan's vanishing. An interesting aside to the story, Morgan supposedly entered into a $500,000 "penal bond" with three other men, in the book deal to publish his expose. Of further interest is the fact that Morgan's Expose "inadvertently" became the standard printed version of the Freemasonic Ritual, used by more Lodge brothers than any other in America throughout the 19ᵗʰ and early 20ᵗʰ centuries!

Hitherto, it was "illegal" according to Masonic Law to print or write the Rituals down. Every degree was to be transmitted orally, in the ancient tradition from "mouth to ear"; therefore, the only printed versions of the rituals available on the book market *were* illegal expose`s! Morgan's was very thorough and accurate, with all the degrees of American Ancient Craft Masonry included, complete with the chivalric orders as well. The three other men were close associates of Morgan's; his landlord being one of them, another man who entered the lodge as Apprentice but never moved further, and the third was the printer publishing the book. It does curiously beg the question of *who* collected the royalties on all those book sales.

The very first alternative political party to Democrats and Republicans in America was the Anti-Masonic Party, which challenged Andrew Jackson's Presidential campaign of 1832, and his administration. Notably, Jackson was a known Freemason, and the only "surviving" President of four in American history, to openly resist the Central Banking system and win; the other three being assassinated in public by gunshot to the head, for their efforts. He was a populist President, a General, and a war hero, though considering the Trail of Tears his was a selective humanitarianism; that savage atrocity was committed on his watch and by *his* command. We will recall as well, the Rev. Pierce from Rochester, NY-run off for suspected Illuminati ties, as well as "Scotch Masons" associates-was appointed the first Minister of Education for Detroit, Michigan's newly-legislated compulsion schooling system. This prototype then legislated and enforced nationwide. It seems many questions could be begged here.

Joseph Smith was from the same 'Burned-Over District' as William Morgan in the Hudson River Valley region in upstate New York. Smith found the famous gold plates, with the Angel Moroni, in nearby Palmyra, New York. In 1830, Lucinda Morgan, widow of William Morgan, who five years before had identified the corpse found in the Niagara River as her husband, moved to the Midwest after marrying George Harris, a silversmith twenty years her senior from nearby Batavia, NY, and there the Harrises became Mormons.

After Joseph Smith was murdered in 1844, Lucinda Morgan Harris was "sealed", a quasi-magickal/masonic ceremony of betrothal to the Father of the LDS Church based on Smith's visionary revelations, also taking on the surname Smith. It is speculated that Smith was quite possibly murdered by Masonic brothers, as Masons were known to criticize many Mormon practices most especially the adoption of Masonic rituals and regalia for "Temple Mormonism"; legend has it there were masonic rings on the fingers of the triggers of the guns that cut Smith down. In 1850 the Harris' separated; George Harris was excommunicated as a lapsed Mormon, and died in 1860. The last report of Lucinda Morgan Harris Smith was from that same year which said she had joined the Catholic Sisters of Charity in Memphis, TN where she worked at the Leah Asylum.

Among the Mormon practices which I have discovered during research into my own family history, was "posthumous baptism", whereby people were taken, after death, into the LDS Church-without their consent-for eternity! All Mormon practices leading to the ultimate goal of apotheosis, which means to become divine. It is a strange coincidence that, in 1841, the Mormons announced their official baptism of William Morgan, 15 years after his disappearance and supposed demise, as one of the first under their new rite to convert the deceased.

We have to wonder what might have been really going on behind the scenes of the whole affair. Who *was* William Morgan? Does it even matter what really happened to him? Does anyone else find it remarkable his last name was Morgan, the same name of one of the biggest names in banking of the 20th century (and 21st), considering his efforts inadvertently helped to derail the only populist President in American history to successful hamper the international bankster-thugs and their white-capped agents of chaos in the Supreme Council 33rd?

According to Wikipedia: "In June 1881 in Pembroke, NY, a grave was discovered in a quarry two miles south of an unidentified Indian Reservation, in it was a metal box containing a crumpled piece of paper; its few legible words were interpreted to indicate the grave was the remains of William Morgan…"

I think it is also important to note here that the Higher Degrees associated with both the York Rite and the Scottish Rite were the main focus of suspicion and derision by the general public of America, the quarrel ultimately being once again not with Freemasonry proper in the abstract, but with the form Masonry had taken after the Revolution. The election cycles as early as 1800 almost cost Jefferson his Presidency, due to the fearful rhetoric saturating the American citizenry that the Government was being overrun, and subverted, by foreign agents of a global illuminati bankster-cabal set on controlling the nation and the world.

It is once again remarkable in that a pattern of having Freemasonry, as a whole, suffer the suspicions, scorn, and condemnation rightfully meant for other operatives and agents of higher degrees, has been consistently employed to divert attention away from those truly responsible. Instead focusing the blame or allowing the blame to be focused on the Blue Lodge of Freemasonry. Time and again, an incident that is potentially dangerous, and generating negative publicity for the fraternity as a whole, is deflected from the true culprits who, upon closer investigation, are invariably "white-capped" operatives of side orders concordant with Freemasonry.

As we have clearly and consistently shown here in this essay, the Ancient York Rite is the complete system of American Craft Masonry; the misunderstanding of the uninitiated leads to the erroneous conclusion that the York Rite is a separate system of so-called higher degrees like the Scottish Rite, when in fact it is the completion of the American Freemasonic education.

10

<u>CONCLUSIONS</u>

So, here we are. At the conclusion to this brief study, this journey; a voyage of exploration to understand the state of affairs in Freemasonry, as I personally found them entering the Lodge. And in this investigational research and review of seemingly endless pages of material, we explored the origins of the York and Scottish Rites of Freemasonry, as well as Ancient Craft Masonry in America itself, along with telling you my own personal tale, which I hope, you found interesting and informative.

Yet we must conclude somehow all we have reviewed and I must inform you what it is that I take away from all this, what I am trying to suggest, imply, and convey to you through the present volume you are reading. Though I have attempted always to hold the rudder fast, and steer straight through the rough waters, swamps, quagmires, and the open sea of materials and references we have navigated with our speculations; no easy task, to be sure.

Yes, I am biased by my own ideals, expectations, and experiences. But I ask you, dear reader, who is not equally biased by such factors as these? How do we as humans divorce such factors from our attempt to be objective and still remain, well, *human*? I have tried to remain as objective as one possibly could, considering the circumstances. And, yes, I distilled the materials studied and reviewed to write this book, often times making difficult choices on what not to include; otherwise the present work might have been 10,000 pages long. It has been an exercise in limitation.

When I began this work, I launched it from the perspective of one in complete support of Freemasonry and its concordant orders, as one who believed Freemasonry might recover its former glory and be redeemed. I believed it might be reinstated as a universal education system for the individual mason, which was its once intended purpose; a Protestant, mystical system of self-help. I was eager to maintain the honor and dignity I imagined the Order still possessed.

Alas, as we reach the end of this examination, I no longer fear depreciating or devaluing the present system of Freemasonry. I could not possibly do more harm than has already been done. I could not damage the honor and dignity of the Order, as it has already been irreparably diminished and devalued, by its own hands, its own leadership; by its own membership.

And since commencing this treatise, more and more research materials have come to light and been brought to my attention, which have served to alter my opinions and intended conclusions with regards to Freemasonry; enough in fact to warrant a second volume on the subject! My main thrust remains-which I believe I have provided substantial proofs from numerous sources-to strongly call into question, and shine new light upon, the validity of claims of authority and tradition made by the Scottish Rite, and most especially its Supreme Council 33rd Degree.

I also succeeded in chronicling honestly and completely my personal experiences inside the Lodge systems. As I have mentioned above, I have most recently become less and less involved in Freemasonry in general. I have all but deactivated my memberships in all orders relating to Freemasonry, aside from maybe the AODA and the BOTA which claim only lateral connections and origins within the Masonic system, both no longer requiring a member to be a Freemason to join and allowing women equal membership status to men. I consider the end of my masonic career to be a great tragedy and I have struggled to accept the outcome of this journey. Though rationally, I know I could never have found a real home in Freemasonry.

I have come to realize the hermetic vision I had so long ago on that cool morning, when that red-tailed hawk frantically clawed at the golden square and compass emblem on the façade of the former Masonic Temple for a place to perch, was not what I thought. The message of the hawk, an ancient symbol of messenger of the gods, seems now to symbolize that my spirit would never be able to truly reside within the Freemasonic Lodge structure. My spirit would instead find a suitable perch in the open air outside the Temple. It has also been suggested that maybe the hawk , a bird of prey representing the lodge of the double-headed eagle or the Scottish Rite was depicting the attack on Freemasonry that I was destined here to defend against.

But still we are left to wonder, with the many details we have unpacked and the many we have not, what is the agenda of Freemasonry today? Many questions persist, with answers no clearer to being perceived than when we began. We are not certain of the motives of many men cast in the vast and elaborate pageant making up the history of the Scottish Rite and Ancient Craft Masonry, nor up to the present day for that matter.

As Nicholas Hagger writes in Chapter 8 of The Secret Founding of America, we can never truly know all the factors motivating key-players from 150-plus years ago…we must focus on results, on the effects of their actions, because while intentions make good road pavement, in the end what *happens* is all that really matters. And while we can never know the true allegiances and loyalties of operatives, their presence and involvement at key points in the timeline chain of events leading up to the present conditions and circumstances today within the Freemasonic system, remain their own indictment.

There are plenty of other indictments to draw from, out of the stacks and reams of pages whether pulp or digital exposing thoughts and words, revealing intentions which we have always feared and suspected. And we will reprint, in the appendices of this volume, several scathing accusations from eye-witness accounts which cannot be thoroughly substantiated based on the nature of the incidents and the people involved; the requests of anonymity by most of those offering testimony out of fear of reprisals and vendetta. They will be reprinted for review and consideration, to offer "equal airtime", as it were, to some of the harsher critics of the fraternity.

There are several rare and obscure tomes which can often be found collecting dust on the shelves of what passes for libraries in most subordinate lodges in America, which offer very interesting insights into the "global view" of the early leadership of the Scottish Rite. The books are a curious group of privately issued volumes under the headings of "Legenda" and "Readings" 1-33. On the surface these books seem to be nothing more than supplemental commentaries to the massive compilation that is Morals and Dogma by Albert Pike; and though the works are unsigned, they were clearly written by a disciple, if not the man himself, in the latter half of the 19th century. I have reviewed all these volumes and possess a few copies myself, especially the 32nd and 33rd of both sets.

Legenda 32 states clearly: "…that the doctrine of Masonry will ultimately rule the intellectual world is certain, though that day is far distant in the future, and Masonry must in the end conquer because its only weapons are truth, charity, and persuasion, and that logic of reason of which the sword of a Knight is the symbol…"[59]

The essential doctrine of the Scottish Rite is laid out in Legenda 19-32 (collected into one volume), which delivers the consistent vision of the S.R. as the great bringer of equilibrium to the masses and calls for the realization of "…a new world order out of chaos …the intellectual and social chaos in the midst of which we perish has for its cause the neglect of initiation of its test and its mysteries." The author of Legenda continues to cite the ills of the uninitiated masses, which lack "the essential law of nature, that of initiation by labors, and of dangerous, toilsome, and voluntary progress, has been fatally disowned …to rebuild society, shattered and decayed we must reestablish hierarchy and initiation.

And this is the great purpose of the Scottish Rite!...The reign of superstition has begun and must endure until the time when the true religion shall be established on the eternal bases of the hierarchy in three degrees, and of the triple power which the ternary exercises fatally and providentially in the three worlds." [60]A discourse on faith and reason, and the law of equilibrium follows on page 102.

We are left to marvel and wonder at these quotes above. What is remarkable, at first, is the focus and mention of only the "hierarchy in 3 degrees", presumably those of the Blue Lodge. The degrees of Ancient Craft Masonry, as we have clearly shown, stand distinctly and completely outside any supposed jurisdiction of the Supreme Council and the Grand Commander of the Scottish Rite, no matter the spurious and extravagant claims made to the contrary. As we have proven beyond doubt, the Scottish Rite is NOT a part of Freemasonry proper, it has NO CLAIM whatsoever to the degrees of Freemasonry in any legal and regular Blue Lodge in the world, only the imaginary powers it vainly imposes.

And still to this day, voices more "educated" and more thoroughly promoted, attempt to rewrite the history and origins of the Scottish Rite, glossing over the York Rite and deliberately misinforming and downplaying the York Rite's significance in the establishment and growth of Ancient Craft Masonry in America.

In 2006, Alpha Books published a book titled The Complete Idiot's Guide to Freemasonry by S. Brent Morris, 33rd degree Supreme Council. Setting aside for a moment the implications of this title for anyone drawn to reading such material, which tellingly insults the reader by its very title, one has to wonder what kind of readership he'd hoped to attract in the first place. I must confess I can be counted among the complete idiots who wasted their time and energy reviewing this so-called guide to Freemasonry, just for the record.

A quick search of Dr. S. Brent Morris online shows he has served as Executive of the Cryptologic Mathematician Program at the National Security Agency, and as U.S. Representative to the International Organization for Standardization (ISO), in the area of computer security. He has taught at the National Cryptologic School as well.

When I met him at Masonic Week 2013, outside of Washington

DC, he did mention, almost immediately upon meeting him, that he was "retired" from the Cryptography Department of-I thought he said-"the CIA." But according to every mention of him online it's the NSA, which he is now retired from. We also discussed his latest work; it seems he was working on a 16th century Masonic cipher he discovered in the archives of the Grand Lodge of England. Never mind the obvious problem such a document would pose to the official timeline of 1717 being the genesis point of English Craft Masonry (and therefore world Freemasonry), what he described to me was a one-letter sigil-cipher encoded with multi-layered characters which he was working on decoding at the time. Borrowing my pocket notebook he drew one on a page, which amounted to several characters stacked on top of each other for each letter in the cipher, which suggested multiple meanings packed into each letter of the cipher. It was fascinating and unusual to me, I had seen nothing like it in any of my Masonic research.

Meeting Dr. Morris was surreal to say the least, because I was under direct orders from my mentors, and the leadership of the Rosicrucian College to which I belong, to keep my head down and "don't attract any attention or stir up any controversy…just go in there get advanced to the next grade and get outta there!" My mentors knew me all too well. They knew if I got to talking with anyone, and revealed my inner thoughts and questions about Freemasonry and other esoteric orders, there was a good chance I might attract unwanted attention and not receive the blessings of the High Council and Supreme Magus, who had final and absolute say on all appointments and advancements.

The Third Order and the High Council of the Rosicrucians contain the two highest grades in the Rosicrucian Colleges: the 8th Grade Magister Templi (Master of the Temple) and the 9th Grade Magus, or "Chief Adept". The hierarchical structure of the Rosicrucian College was, in fact, very much like the Scottish Rite Supreme Council and Vatican Papal power structures, and *unlike* the more democratic structure of the orders of Ancient Craft Masonry. S. Brent Morris is a Chief Adept. I chatted with him outside the fancy high ceiling ballroom at the Hyatt Regency, awaiting entrance into the "Mystic Circle" where several of us would advance to the 8th Grade and be made members of the High Council. I was being advanced in order to serve as Secretary of the local College of Rosicrucians to which I belonged.

The ritual of advancement was very impressive and, in my opinion, the most "magically" arranged and oriented of any of the Masonic rituals or ceremonies I have experienced; having been initiated into 9 Masonic Orders including the three degrees of the Blue Lodge, the 3 bodies of the York Rite-the Chapter, Council, and Commandery, the Order of the Allied Masonic Degrees, also the Order of the Knight Masons, the SRICF (or Rosicrucian College) which has 9 Grades, the Order of the Sword of Bunker Hill, the Builders of the Adytum (or BOTA), and the Ancient Order of Druids in America of which I have advanced to Druid Apprentice amounting to 2 degrees, all Masonic in origin and structure.

Those of us who were advancing to the 8th Grade of Magister Templi stood, with arms interlocked, within the main ballroom of the Hyatt Regency, complete with "Tiffany Glass"-looking chandeliers, next to Dulles Airport in DC; all of us in tuxedos forming a circle around the altar with a large group of Chief Adepts from all the States, as well as foreign nations, looking on outside the ring of Aspirants. Within the circle, at the Altar, was the Celebrant officiating the ceremony and looking remarkably like the Magician of the Tarot Deck, with all the same tools on the altar, including cup, wooden wand, circle and pentacle.

The Frater to my immediate left was none other than Masonic author Christopher Hodapp, who has penned a series of slanted (towards the Scottish Rite of course) and over-simplified works the so-called "Masonry for Dummies" series. I did briefly chat with him as well, though once again I (regrettably) followed orders from my home College leadership not to engage in any controversy, concealing my opinions regarding the Scottish Rite and the state of modern Freemasonry in general.

I crossed paths with the "evil emperor" Secretary General from the AMD fiasco, with not a word about the incident passing between us. I shook hands with the then Grand Master of the Grand Encampment of Knights Templar of America, who is also the Supreme Magus of the SRICF (Rosicrucian Colleges in America). I also met the Grand Commander of the Grand Commandery of Romania, the Grand Master of the Grand Priory of Canada, the Supreme Magus of the SRIS (Rosicrucian Colleges in Scotland), and scores of other dignitaries including government officials in the mayor's office in DC and who knows what other departments and agencies really. It was all very daunting to say the least.

Let us now return to Morris' Complete Idiot's Guide, and consider the implications of this title. I guess the joke is lost on me, or maybe the subject matter is far more serious and important to me than to Dr. Morris and his publishers. Unlike Dr. Morris, I have more faith in my readership or at the very least hold you all in higher esteem, than to call you "complete idiots" or "dummies". On closer examination of the contents of this so-called "guide", we find blatant falsehoods, pure propaganda, disinformation, and misinformation.

Material taken from Morris' Guide, which is published on the official Scottish Rite website under the heading "History of the Rite", makes many outrageous and blatantly disrespectful claims and boasts. He sets the stage by stating, right away, that the early history of Freemasonry and the origins of the Scottish Rite are "hidden in mist".

Next he attempts to establish some sort of authority and tradition for the Scottish Rite by invoking the legendary "Scotch Masons" or "Scots Master Masons" and supposed evidence (unproduced) claiming these notorious Masons were already operating in England as early as 1730, which is contrary to our findings. Capitalizing on his assumption that he is dealing with "complete idiots", he counts on none of his readers knowing how the Scotch Masons behaved inside the Blue lodge; nor how the governing bodies of Freemasonry in Europe were eventually forced to pass legislation limiting the despotic, and elitist, practices and prerogatives of these so-called "Scot Master Masons", due to abuses and widespread complaints within the Fraternity, regarding their conduct. Just as with the claimed lineage tracing back to Frederick the Great; the average uninformed reader would likely be impressed by this "claim to fame"; while ignorant, of the fact that Frederick was known to have been an unsavory leader, to say the least. Are these the kind of people one would claim proudly as progenitors?

He then goes on to casually dismiss the York Rite out of hand, in the first of many shots taken against the clearly elder, and more august, order. He points out that, a couple of years after the Grand Lodge of France restricted the Scotch Masons powers within the Blue Lodge System, they received even more special privileges and authority, from 1747-1755, which only goes to show their methods were working-and that those of influence, recruited into their camps, had done their "due diligence". He tells his readers, "…in contrast, the Royal Arch (and the York Rite by default!) 'appears' in lodge minutes in America and England in 1758 with little official notice". How incredibly degrading and disrespectful, and completely ignorant, this statement truly is!

It seems Dr. Morris would have his readers imagine a fantastic, mythological lineage between the modern Scottish Rite and a bunch of elitist operatives from a completely different system in Europe half a century before, while at the same time ignoring D'Assigny's mention of the Royal Arch being worked in the British Isles in 1744, even though in the matter-of-fact way its mentioned in a paper quoted at the beginning of this treatise, it was universally accepted and already a tradition integral to the Craft Masonry system. We are left wondering how Morris, along with the rest of the Scottish Rite gang, gives little credence to something "…with little official notice…" that was considered important enough to mention *specifically* in the famous Constitutions of the United Grand Lodge of England in 1813; that "…pure Antient (ancient) Masonry consists of 3 degrees…and also including the Supreme Order of the Holy Royal Arch", and still no official mention of the Scottish Rite, or the Rite of Perfection, whatsoever. Huh…

He also confirms what we already learned, that early continental degree systems-as well as Freemasonry proper-sought to attract the upper classes and nobility. He makes it clear how classist in nature the development of European masonry truly was, and is. Next, he contributes to the cacophony of baseless and unsubstantiated claims made with regards to the immigration of the infamous and overrated Morin Patent, and the man himself to the New World. One statement which seems an honest indictment of Morin, rather than endorsement, is made when he claims that Morin "…apparently acted to create a new Masonic body with himself as the only Grand Inspector." Even though we know that was not what the genuine Morin Patent clearly stated as his powers.

We have already seen how, 'for a small fee', each Inspector General could confer degrees, establish new bodies, and make new Inspectors at will. Even Morris tells us "there were no guidelines on cost, no limitation of numbers, and no restriction on how many more Inspectors any one Inspector could create. By 1800 there were over 80 Inspector Generals and the system was moving toward chaos…"

Next, one learns in this quasi-history that the itinerant degree peddling we described above, practiced by the Continental system was seen as a "good thing"; in that, unlike the "English York Rite", these French degrees were spread by travelling inspectors peddling their pseudo-masonic degrees for profit. Masons no longer had to wait for charter applications and proper channels to receive higher degrees in that the transient Inspectors "could take care of everything as soon as he arrived…" presumably however he saw fit. How very convenient...

Meanwhile in the UK and America, Ancient Craft Masonry,

including the York Rite, was far surpassing this frenzy of pseudo-masonic orders vying for authority and control in membership and tradition; establishing its own traditions with the authority of a true lineage. Dr. Morris makes the outright false claim that the first Supreme Council of the 33rd degree declared its existence in 1801(!); completely ignoring the documented prehistory of the Scottish Rite, Ineffable Degrees, and multiple Supreme Councils *before* the 1801 incarnation. This new Supreme Council boastfully declared control of the "higher degrees" in America as the so-called "mother council of the world", only to be ignored, even laughed at, by real Craft Masonry worldwide. This newly invented organization seemed then to fold in on itself like the flimsy house of cards it really was. It dwindled into almost complete obscurity for the next half a century until its "savior" General Albert Pike appeared on the scene.

As we have examined, the Supreme Council's authority was and is based on bogus claims of history, propped up by imaginary Templar/Chivalric origins combined with real nobility recruited to lend authenticity and legitimacy to the organization. With hubris and ambition, he tells us the 1801 Supreme Council is ancestor to all other regular and lawful Supreme Councils today.

I could go on like this indefinitely dissecting Dr. Morris' entire history. I could fill a book with my rebuttals of his guide, and maybe I will another time. For now, his guide for complete idiots would have just as soon gone unmentioned in this study, being part of the vast catalog of misinformation and disinformation sources out there were it not for the remarkable fact that the guide is actively being adopted nationwide by Grand Lodges in America as the official curriculum for Masonic Education!

I would now recall my last visit to the Grand Lodge of my "home" Masonic jurisdiction, a region with nearly 2 centuries of York Rite tradition and also where I was dubbed a Knight Templar.

Like some tragic final act in a Greek play, I will drive home my point here; several months ago, as of this present writing, I was coerced by a Past Grand Commander of the Grand Commandery of Knights Templar, to accompany him at a Grand Lodge of Research business meeting. It was obviously an attempt on his part to retain my active involvement in Masonry especially Masonic Education, and as I was technically still a member of the Lodge of Research I complied. I went mostly out of loyalty to the Grand Commander. I had not attended a Lodge of Research meeting in years due to my realization that it was a flagrant waste of my time and effort. The meeting, in point of fact, had the opposite effect than what he intended, to be sure.

In this particular meeting, the business at hand was the hostile take-over of the Lodge of Research, originally created to educate masons statewide properly through research and review of the extensive three-tiered library housed within the sizable stone Grand Lodge structure for paper-writing and peer evaluation, by the most recent Past Grand Master of the State, in order to bring the organization under the newly formed superfluous bureaucracy called the Council of Administration-populated exclusively by the political "jet-set" of high ranking members of the Grand Lodge leadership, most of who were also high-ranking Scottish Rite members.

This surplus council was obviously established to subvert and circumvent the already completely formed political system within the Grand Lodge. It was clearly a coup; a power grab. There was a circling of wagons going on with all the committees and organizations within the Grand Lodge system. A restructuring was underway, and the current top officers in the "Grand Line" were depicted on the cover of the most recent State masonic periodical in Traditional Grand Lodge Masonic Regalia under the heading, "VIVA LA REVOLUCION"(!); just *what* this revolution is that they refer to remains unclear.

The topper was when the Past Grand Master, leading the coup within the Lodge of Research, declared that the Scottish Rite was the "only answer to all the problems plaguing Freemasonry today", most especially the lack of masonic Education. I knew I had enough. This marauder walked into the meeting; impeccably dressed like the corporate CEO he just happened to be, with a smug air of disdain all over him. When given the floor, he told us he "just happened to stop by" and "had no intention of running for office of Master of the Lodge." Yet, once nominated, he produced a very polished campaign address which he expertly delivered to the Lodge. It was very impressive as well as repugnant.

The worst moment was when he asked the room, "What's a Master Mason to do, in any given Blue Lodge, when he finds himself lacking a proper Masonic Education after being raised to the 3rd degree?" You could have heard a pin drop. I looked frantically around the room at several high ranking prestigious York Rite Masons with decades of service to the fraternity servants everyone, some of the very same Guardians of the Grail who had shown me the path to truth so long ago, and I was shocked and dismayed. Because I knew, as they all did, the most obvious answer to the rhetorical question that the Past Grand Master certainly didn't want uttered was, "He should join the York Rite and complete his proper Masonic education!"

But no one said a word. They all sat there in silent acquiescence. And sitting there heart-broken, I too remained silent, burning with my own shame and regret. I looked around the room and stared into the eyes of every man who would meet my gaze, and realized it was hopeless. That all these men, the only ones with the power to change a thing, would rather sit in indifferent cowardly silence than risk any amount of political backlash and effect their "legacy" however that might serve anyone.

The final straw came when I asked the Past Grand Master how he proposed to meet the education needs, specifically of area Masons, what would be the source material? I was informed the source materials would be the recently adopted statewide Masonic Education system, developed directly from S. Brent Morris' Complete Idiot's Guide to Freemasonry! It was the coup de grace, and with that all hopes were dashed. This secret war we have been addressing suffered a crushing defeat that day.

The sting of that moment demoralizes me even with these words. And on an even sadder note, I must report that Freemasonry in general is not doing well, aside from pockets of affluence and exceptions. The Blue Lodge, York Rite and Scottish Rite orders in my area are suffering their lowest attendance and negative growth in membership ever recorded since their establishment in the territory, as are all the other concordant orders across the nation. And of these, the stated communications (official monthly meetings) barely met the required quorum to open for business; and all of them had little or no new members initiated, or even planning on initiating any time soon.

As an aside, the York Rite body I belong to recently received a new petition for membership from a Master Mason in a neighboring city and was barely able to initiate the man; only four members of the York Rite participated, all of them playing several parts in the ritual in spite of the fact that over ten times as many men are "qualified", being members, to perform the ritual initiation of new members, though lacking in the "proficiency" to do so.

One of the most heart-breaking aspects to all this is the disappointment of literally scores of sincere committed brothers who have served the fraternity most of their adult lives, paying their dues and

116

through active participation, all seemingly for naught. The let-down is palpable. In the final analysis though, as we have gone to great lengths to consider, the journey through the degrees into the "Holy of Holies" within the Western Esoteric Lodge systems is an individual one! And the Aspirant, as a condensed focal point of awareness within cosmic consciousness, has always been and will always be the center of the universe, as all the Hermetic teachings have indicated; therefore the experience of the individual is the paramount goal, enhanced by all the key players and participants in the drama along the way.

If we remain committed to our own growth and development, no one can take away or diminish the experiences we go through. This, in the end, is the final hope we can rest on as a Universal Law of Consciousness: in the end no one can take your growth away from you. They can't even touch it. It is woven into the fabric of your experience. And we who yearn for more light, for the rich inner life available to all, will persist until the water of our life flows back to the source, only to return once more...

So mote it be.

AFTERWARDS

There is much we did not touch upon with regards to other aspects of the thesis we have put forth in these pages. There are many more dimensions to the story and the picture it paints in our minds, the implications that are not provable per se, but we intuit and infer nonetheless. After all, "conspiracy theories" abound, going to the most fantastic and outrageous extremes of speculation, substantiated or not.

Late in the writing of this book I came into contact with one Dr. Colin Ross from Dallas/Fort Worth area psychiatric services-specializing in Satanic Ritual Abuse and Multiple Personality Disorders. Dr. Ross divulged to me during an interview on my podcast that upon reviewing 15,000 pages of declassified CIA MK-Ultra documents he discovered the Scottish Rite Foundation (a charitable organization arm of the fraternal order) was listed among the many corporate financial contributors to numerous CIA front programs. These programs were run by social engineering think-tanks like the Rand Corporation and SRI International Center for the Study of Social Policy-all in the name of MK-Ultra mind control research!

The question MUST be asked: why the Scottish Rite Foundation saw the need to be involved in such research? What dog did they have in the fight? Why would the Scottish Rite be so interested in the specific research of Rand Corp and SRI International?

The Grand Commander of the Supreme Council Henry Clausen before he retired in the mid-1980's wrote an interesting little book called: "Your Amazing Mystic Powers" which described his official visits (as Grand Commander of the Scottish Rite and therefore head administrator of the Scottish Rite Foundation) to various government funded "research facilities" run by Rand and SRI. He spoke proudly of the cutting edge "paranormal" and "psychic" research being conducted (under the MK-Ultra banner that is) to further scientific achievement and development.

The man who would succeed Clausen was one C. Fred Kleinknect. A rising star in the Supreme Council during the 60's and 70's he served as the Secretary General, and eventually assumed the throne of the double-headed eagle becoming its Grand Commander in 1985.

Remarkably, Kleinknect's brother Kenneth (also a 33rd degree Inspector General) was the Apollo Space Program Manager all during the lunar missions of the 60's and 70's. Of course every one of the Lunar

Astronauts were members of the Scottish Rite.

SRI stands for Stanford Research Institute. This government think-tank extraordinaire is responsible among other things for producing the 1974 report titled: "Changing Images of Man" which predicted a wide-spread awakening and broadening of consciousness all throughout America (and worldwide) sometime around the turn of the millennium 2000-2001. The study indicated this would cause instability in all markets and chaos in the establishment. The citizens of America would finally question the authority which had controlled their society.

Traditional forms of social structure and control would be made obsolete by this awakening. Something had to be done. The social scientists and engineers over at SRI mapped out several plans, programs, and methods for derailing and diverting this awakening. Included among the designs for corralling our collective consciousness, listed like an afterthought in the appendices of the report was the employment of symbolism and emblematic devices to captivate and "entrain" the modern American mind. Material consumerism the focused core value of American progress would be triggered and reinforced every step of personal development.

As the culture steadily approached the country's bicentennial, specifically Egyptian iconography and Masonic symbols and themes were suggested by the study to be most effective in penetrating the American psyche to activate the civic mythology dormant within. The myth of democratic progress, free enterprise, and manifest destiny are powerful forces woven deep into the fabric of American social identity.

These would be the continued ideals of the 'new age" a new world order. The principle pillars of the great American social experiment.

Not unlike the work of public relations pioneer Edward Bernays and his 1928 playbook on social policy manipulation called: Propaganda, the Changing images of Man report calls for the employment of ALL methods of communication and telecommunications as well as civic and social organizations, arts and entertainment, to sculpt and craft public perception most especially 'mass consciousness" as a unique singular entity susceptible to suggestion and "trusted leaders" to guide and coerce the beast.

And I can't help but wonder and suspect that the root cause of my personal preoccupation with all things Freemasonic may not have been of my own design, but a conditioned response implanted through multi-media and cultural suggestion grafted to my awareness. And of course we can't ignore the blatant saturation of all forms of media for the last 40 years with the very symbolism prescribed in the SRI report. We know there is an imbalance in our society-a cognitive dissonance that permeates everyday awareness: the generation gap, the war between the sexes, racial strife and tensions, the celebration of "diversity" leaving only dissent, division, and exclusion. Divided we fall as a culture, as a people: *ethne* from the Greek. All these forms of cognitive dissonance, vibrational frequency discord.

Fear, anxiety, and sexual desire are the fertile lands upon which our modern sorcerers of media magic reinforce the memes and paradigms through suggestion and misdirection-for the successful harvest of total mind-control. Mind control coming in many forms some more harmless than others-like the civic myths perpetrated in our societies-the collective story of us.

Deliberate government fabrication of public consensus raises alarms at a whole different level. Considering the Scottish Rite funding of government think-tanks, Grand Commander Clausen's book on "amazing mystic powers", the most important members of the Apollo space missions all sworn allegiance to the Supreme Council 33rd Degree of the Scottish Rite (even Tranquility Lunar Lodge #2000 bears its charter!); we marvel at the implications of all this.

If we continue to expand the scope beyond merely the borders of the United States we can consider the position and contentions posited by Brother James Wright contained within the appendices of this work. His perspective adding an international dimension to the Scottish Rite assumption of authority and tradition, the continued machinations to suppress facts and rewrite histories to serve their worldview and agenda.

And what might this agenda be? And what be the results of all this? As always with much in life, it depends on your particular perspective whether it has all led to chaos or accord, for my part it seems clear, in the immortal words spoken in the Gospels: "...you will know them by their fruits..." or as I like to say what's in the well comes out in the bucket!

In the process of preparing this book I interviewed, debriefed, and interrogated many people connected to or members of the various bodies and side orders affiliated with Freemasonry in America and worldwide. Much of what was divulged to me in these sessions is not contained within this book as either unrelated or unprovable hearsay or I was sworn to secrecy by those witnessed to things or directly involved.

Some things left me troubled with more questions to answer than when I started. And I come away from all of this realizing that contrary to my former belief that most of the stories and legends about 'satanic cults" in America are just that; I know now there are much more to these stories and rumors than urban legends. Although I never personally witnessed anything remotely like the kind of activities to which I refer, it was revealed to me by a very trusted source, one of the "guardians of the grail" to whom I made mention, in fact!

During just such a debriefing about a year and a half before the publication of this book I was given a startling revelation.
My principle mentor and brother Mason was a high ranking Past Master of many State level bodies in the Mid-West-a man of high regard and some prestige and repute among his fellows, very active in his local church, he was also active in many other civic and municipal activities and occupations as well-even at post retirement age. I must admit he had great influence on the course of my masonic education early on, as well as, my choices of affiliation within the orders. I considered him a man of great character and intentions.

I often felt awkward discussing the darker aspects of magic and masonry thinking him to be too "pure of heart" and good natured to fathom the shadows of reality. He was a source of much insight and inside information as a lifetime member and witness to many misdeeds conducted within the lodge system. I spent many hours sitting on his porch with a digital audio recorder takings notes.

One day after we were talking about various side orders like the mysterious Ancient Order of Toltec out of Topeka, Kansas, that once peppered the landscape of America when he matter-of-factly made the remark, "Well I already told you about my being involved with that Satanic Coven that met on the full moon back in the 60's and 70's way out in the country out by the old haunted church and cemetery in Stull, Kansas…"

I almost fell out of my chair because I had, in fact, *never* heard any such thing from him, which I assured him as I pressed him for more details! He then just as blatantly recounted to me tales of a sister who was sensitive to occult things often using the Ouija board and Tarot cards to divine with. He told me how she had shown him to use them to converse with spirits. And one day while using the Tarot cards, Satan himself appeared before my brother mason. He described the devil as being in multicolored form beyond anything he had ever seen. Satan commanded him to fall down and worship that he "…may receive the whole wide world…"

He assured me that he refused the devil's bargain and that he quit his evils ways-of course not before attending "…many full moon rituals with other men, women, and animals doing unmentionable things in the pale moonlight…"

Needless to say, I was left very perplexed by these admissions.

As The Bard said:

"There are many things in heaven and earth Horatio, than are dreamt of in your philosophies…"

But that, as they say, is another story…

Frater X   12-07-14

APPENDIX

My Vantage Point of the Masonic Wars
By James Robert Wright, 32° KT

When I was an administrative employee of the Scottish Rite of Freemasonry's Supreme Council, it came to my attention early on of various elements between the York and Scottish Rite which spoke of a conspiracy inside the Scottish to hijack and bankrupt the York out of existence, in order that the Scottish Rite may in the future control all of Freemasonry and confer all Degrees 1 to 33.

That being said, my conclusion of this very real conspiracy is that it, in and of itself, is actually irrelevant to the true war going on. Growing up in a family composed of Spencers, de Veres, Viscontis, Saint-Clairs, Plantagenets, Hamiltons and Stewarts (just to name a few) and coming into the world in a certain clan with deep roots laid in Texas whose vast wealth came from building the original media empire Texas ever started with, and those same family members being active 33rd Degree board members in the Scottish Rite, I have had nothing but elite elbow-rubbing my entire life, whether I seek it out or not.

Having lived a life like this so far, I absolutely conclude beyond any shadow of a doubt that everything the public has been told about the origins of Freemasonry are boldfaced lies. Not only that, everything we were all fed in grade school about European History and "King Arthur and his Round Table of Knights" are equally erroneous; clever forgeries intended to confuse and pollute the world with the sort of disinformation necessary for the rogue element that is the Scottish Rite to further hijack and control the rights to this ancient tradition.

The real story, in a nutshell is as follows:

Once upon a time Freemasonry, the Vatican, and monarchies alike were all administered by a group known, historically, as the "Knights Templar". This elite 'Jedi-like' group with international diplomatic immunity was, for all intents and purposes, the 'moral police' of the entire planet. Their job, from the moment of their inception by the families forming the original Priory of Sion, was to exist as a Council for the people whom policed the corruption inside the world's institutions.

123

Consequently, on October 13, 1307, they were done in by a conspiracy originating in France and the Vatican to undermine and destroy the Templars and thusly erase their patrol from vice and corruption in politics. In the heat of this tragedy, a plan was devised to take the Templars' wealth and information underground and protect it, and in so doing concealing it under this new concept of "Freemasonry". Interestingly enough, one passage in their own history books seems to have survived which states, "The Saint-Clairs are the hereditary protectors of Craft Masonry". When I reminded the Grand Lodge of Texas of this fact during their attempt to bring me up on charges of un-Masonic conduct of "criticizing Freemasonry both publically and privately", the charges were curiously dropped.

You see, once upon a time there was a well-known racial subgroup of Caucasians known as the "Merovingians", a.k.a. "Sicambrian Franks", whose job it was to produce the future generations of these Templars, from which they had all originated. It is rather pointless to discuss the origins of this race in this context, or to humor the various slander present put out by none other than Scottish Rite Masons whom seek to continue this centuries old tradition of trying to retain the rights to something that actually does not belong to them. You can equate it to asking a neighbor to watch your children while you run off to war, only to return and find that the neighbor absconded and kidnapped your child.

Freemasonry was originally designed in medieval history to serve as conservators of this power and tradition, and still to this day [the Scottish Rites] are doing everything they can to retain and abuse it. Any abuses perpetrated against its members by its administrators should, for all intents and purposes, be considered as blasphemies, and those perpetrators as charlatans.

I find no need to sugarcoat or conceal what I see and know and hear is coming. There exists a quiet movement in the world today, in all walks of life, by the descendants of these families who were themselves persecuted and genocided by these same dark individuals, whom wish to force the return of the Templar and true "Masonic" symbolic material to its rightful owners. This is no small group of people and quite a lot are affected by it, whether they yet know it or not. These families have come together under the orchestration of the Priory of Sion, a.k.a. Dragon Court a.k.a. Order of the Dragon, to facilitate this happening.

There is going to come a time, sooner than later, when these families rally to serve the Scottish Rite with a complete cease-and-desist class action suit, demanding their immediate halt to profiting and continued usurping of these once very wholesome and Christian Gnostic traditions, which have now been perverted by them into Luciferian doctrine. Just ask Albert Pike, the modern day re-organizer of the Scottish Rite, who was nothing more than an obese, deranged and treasonous pervert. He may not be alive to answer anymore, but at least the House of the Temple keeps his mummified corpse on hand in Washington D.C. to play with in the 31st Degree of Inspector Inquisitor as a stage prop, a.k.a. 'necromancy'.

If one awakens to the reality of the situation going on between these orders-and I mean all of them, including but not limited to all current active sects of Freemasonry, Rosicrucianism, Ordo Templi Orientis, Golden Dawn, Silver Star (Illuminati) etc. etc., then one must disregard the vicious lies put forth by the trashy fantasy history books that have enveloped modern society like a vicious plague. Anybody interested in further examination should study the works of some of the true recent greats of our time, such as Martin Lunn, Prince Nicholas de Vere of Hungary, and Sir Laurence Gardner.

This war I speak of has caused the demise of some very beautiful and illustrious people, such as Princess Diana Spencer, Prince Nicholas de Vere, and others whose lives were terminated by Masonic-run Western intelligence community hit squads. As a cousin to Diana and Nick's apprentice, I will forever be infuriated with these injustices and fight them until my end. Freemasonry has come to know me as the problem that won't go away, as I have vowed to not go quietly and to seek rational solutions to return these traditions to the people and of the people, completely transparent and moral as they were originally intended to be. The biggest lie of Freemasonry is that there is a need for secrecy. This is a lie only spoken by men whom seek to do diabolical things in the shadows, away from the view of the light. Given that there are currently five million active Freemasons in America alone, this is no small or trivial matter and will ultimately affect the entire whole of humanity.

I pray that I myself am able to live long enough to see this reversal set into motion and these usurpers brought to justice.

Sir James Robert Wright   June 2, 2014 Los Angeles, California

FOOTNOTES

CHAPTER TWO:
1) The History of Freemasonry by Robert Freke Gould
2) Vol. 4, p. 614-615 The History of Freemasonry
3) Vol. 4, p. 614 The History of Freemasonry
4) Vol. 4, p. 616 The History of Freemasonry
5) Vol. 4, p. 625 The History of Freemasonry
6) Vol. 4, p. 625 The History of Freemasonry
7) Vol. 4, p. 626 The History of Freemasonry
8) Vol. 4, The History of Freemasonry
9) Vol. 1, p. 285 Freemasonry Through Six Centuries by Henry W. Coil, Sr.
10) Vol. 1, p.286 Freemasonry Through Six Centuries
11) Vol.2, Ch.7, p.350 Freemasonry Through Six Centuries
12) Pt 2, p.197; The American Rite of Freemasonry; The History of the Ancient and Honorable Fraternity of Free and Accepted Masons and Concordant Orders
13) Vol. 2, p.699 Freemasonry Through Six Centuries
14) Vol. 2, p.701 Freemasonry Through Six Centuries

CHAPTER THREE

15) p.271 The Secret Tradition in Freemasonry by A.E. Waite
16) p.503 The Secret Tradition in Freemasonry, Waite
17) (p.503 footnote) The Secret Tradition in Freemasonry by A.E. Waite
18) p.512-513 The Secret Tradition in Freemasonry, Waite
19) p.143 The Secret Tradition in Freemasonry, Waite
20) (p.151) The Secret Tradition in Freemasonry, Waite
21) p.153 The Secret Tradition in Freemasonry, Waite
22) p. 620 The Secret Tradition in Freemasonry, Waite
23) p. 278 The Secret Tradition in Freemasonry, Waite
24) p.442 The Secret Tradition in Freemasonry, Waite
25) Chapter 8, The Secret Founding of America, Nicholas Hagger
26) Nicholas Hagger, The Secret Founding of America

CHAPTER FOUR

27) John Lamb Lash from metahistory.org
28) The Sync Books Volumes 1&2
29) Pt 1, Chap. 2, p.43, The Underground History of American Education by John Taylor Gatto
30) Pt 2, Chap. 7, p.138-9 The Underground History... John Taylor Gatto
31) Part 2, Chap. 7, p.139 The Underground History... John Taylor Gatto
32) Part 2, Chap. 7, p.139-140 The Underground History... John T. Gatto
33) Part 2, Chap. 7, p.140 The Underground History... John Taylor Gatto
34) Part 2, Chap. 7, p.144 The Underground History... John Taylor Gatto
35) Part 2, Chap. 5, p.106 The Underground History... John Taylor Gatto
36) Part 2, Chap. 6, p.121 The Underground History... John Taylor Gatto
37) Part 2, chap. 6, p.128 The Underground History...John Taylor Gatto
38) Part 2, chap. 6, p.126 The Underground History...John Taylor Gatto
39) Part 1, Chap. 7, p.144 The Underground History... John Taylor Gatto
40) Part 2, Chap. 7, p.144 The Underground History... John Taylor Gatto

CHAPTER FIVE

41) Wikipedia entry, Old Prussians, http://en.wikipedia.org/wiki/Old_Prussians
42) Thomas Babington Macaulay (1800-1859), via The Underground History of American Education by John Taylor Gatto, Pt 2, Chap 7 p.136
43) Johann Wolfgang von Goethe (1749-1832), historian, via The Underground History... by John Taylor Gatto, Pt 2, Chapter 7 p.136
44) Pt. 2, Chap. 7, p. 136 The Underground History... John Taylor Gatto
45) Hans Rosenberg (1904-1988), historian, via Underground History... by John Taylor Gatto, Part 2, Chapter 7 p.141
46) Part 2, Chap. 7, p. 140-41, The Underground History... John Taylor Gatto
47) Pg.12 The Masonic Textbook (1855) Jeremy Ladd Cross
48) Chap 17 p. 349, Freemasonry Through Six Centuries by Henry W. Coil, Sr
49) Freemasonry Through Six Centuries by Henry W. Coil, Sr
50) Volume 2, p. 357, Freemasonry Through Six Centuries by Henry W. Coil, Sr

CHAPTER SIX
51) Excerpt from The Lost Keys of Freemasonry by Manly Palmer Hall

CHAPTER SEVEN

52) Excerpt from forward, "The Meaning of Masonry" by Walter Leslie Wilmshurst (1927)
53) P.11-12, The Meaning of Masonry by Walter Leslie Wilmshurst.
54) P. 17, The Meaning of Masonry, Walter L. Wilmshurst
55) P. 111   "   "   "
56) P. 113   "   "   "
57) P. 24, excerpt from "Guide to the Royal Arch Chapter" by James Gould

CHAPTER NINE
58) Excerpt from first footnote in Freemasonry Through Six Centuries by Henry Coil

CHAPTER TEN
59) p. 33, Legenda 32, anonymous, Legenda and Readings of the Ancient and Accepted Scottish Rite of Freemasonry
60) p. 100-101, Legenda 19-30, single volume set, anonymous

BIBLIOGRAPHY/REFERENCES

- Referenced websites: www.dcpages.com/, Oklahoma York Rite www.okyorkrite.org/, www.scottishrite.org/about/history/, John Lamb Lash www.metahistory.org/, Builders of the Adytum (BOTA) www.bota.org/, The Ancient Order of Druids in America (AODA) www.aoda.org/, Max Igan www.thecrowhouse.com/
- The Complete Idiots Guide to Freemasonry by S. Brent Morris
- Albert Pike's Esoterika - The Symbolism of the Blur Degrees of Freemasonry by Arturo De Hoyos
- Albert Pike:
    - -Morals and Dogma
    - - Lectures on Masonic Symbolism and A Second Lecture on Symbolism or the Omkara and other Ineffable Words
- Freemasonry Through Six Centuries by Henry W. Coil, Sr., Volume 1 & 2
- Indiana Cryptic Monitor of Freemasonry
- History of Freemasonry by Robert F. Gould, Volumes 1-6
- The Ancient and Accepted Scottish Rite in 33 Degrees by Robert Folger
- Illustrations of Freemasonry Part 1 &2 by Thomas Smith Webb
- Jeremy Ladd Cross; General Grand Council of Royal Select Masons, International:
    - -True Masonic Chart or Hieroglyphic Monitor
    - -The Masonic Textbook
    - -The Ineffable Degrees
- A Serious and Impartial Inquiry Into the Cause of the Present Decay of Free-Masonry in the Kingdom of Ireland by Fifield D'Assigny
- The History of the Ancient and Honorable Fraternity of Free and Accepted Masons and Concordant Orders, copyright and revised by Lee C. Hascall
- Arthur Edward Waite:
    - -The Secret Tradition in Freemasonry
    - -New Encyclopedia of Freemasonry
- Transcendental Magic: Its Doctrine and Ritual by Eliphas Levi, trans. by A.E. Waite
- The Secret War on Human Consciousness by Frater X, Paranoia Magazine, Fall 2013
- The Secret Founding of America by Nicholas Hagger

- In the Shadow of the Sentinel by Bob Brewer
- John Taylor Gatto:
    - -The Underground History of American Education
    - -Dumbing Us Down
- Manly P. Hall:
    - -The Lost Keys of Freemasonry
    - -The Secret Teachings of All Ages
    - -The Secret Destiny of America
    - -Lectures on Ancient Philosophy: An Introduction to the Study and Application of Rational Procedure
- Creative Mythology by Joseph Campbell
- Not In His Image by John Lamb Lash
- Listen, Little Man by Wilhelm Reich
- The Kybalion by Three Initiates
- The Key to Solomon's Key: Secrets of Magic and Masonry by Lon Milo Duquette
- Wicca for the Solitary Practitioner by Scott Cunningham
- Albert Mackey:
    - -The Masonic Ritual, pocket book
    - -An Encyclopedia of Freemasonry and its Kindred Sciences
- The Meaning of Masonry by Walter Leslie Wilmshurst
- Inside the Magical Lodge by John Michael Greer
- Paul Foster Case:
    - -Occult Fundamentals and Spiritual Unfoldment, Vol. 1: The Early Writings
    - -Esoteric Secrets of Meditation and Magic – Vol. 2: The Early Writings
    - -The Masonic Letter "G"
- Guide to The Royal Arch Chapter by James Gould
- Lodge of the Double Headed Eagle by William Fox
- Stephen Dafoe:
    - -Morgan: The Scandal That Shook Freemasonry
    - - Compasses and the Cross
- Tim Wallace Murphy:
    - -Hidden Wisdom: Secrets of the Western Esoteric System
    - -Templars in America; co-written with Marilyn Hopkins
    - -Cracking the Symbol Code
- The Alchemical Keys to the Masonic Ritual by Timothy Hogan
- The Shadow of Solomon by Laurence Gardiner

- The Dragon Legacy by Prince Nicholas DeVere
- Joseph P. Farrell:
    - Babylon's Banksters
    - Nazi International
- C.H. Claudy:
    - The Master's Book
    - Introduction to Freemasonry, Volumes 1-3
- Secrets of Freemasonry by Robert Lomas
- Christopher Knight and Robert Lomas:
    - The Second Messiah: Templars, the Turin Shroud and the Great Secret of Freemasonry
    - Hiram's Key
- John J. Robinson:
    - Dungeon, Fire and Sword: The Knights Templar in the Crusades
    - Born in Blood
- Ahimon Rezon by Laurence Dermott
- The Builders by Joseph Fort Newton
- Freemasonry and the Ancient Gods by J.S.M. Ward
- A Guide to the Royal Arch Chapter by John Sheville and James L. Gould
- Founding Fathers, Secret Societies: Freemasons, Illuminati, Rosicrucians and the Decoding of the Great Seal by Robert R. Hieronimus
- A History of Royal Arch Masonry: Issued under Authority of the General Grand Chapter Royal Arch Masons by Everett R. Turnbull and Ray V. Denslow
- A Handbook for Royal Arch Masons by Ray Denslow
- Duncan's Rituals by Malcolm Duncan
- Vest Pocket Trestle Board and Working Tools of Symbolic Freemasonry by C.P. Boon
- Freemason's Companion by John Caldwell
- The Temple and the Lodge by Michael Baigent and Richard Leigh
- Freemasonry and Its Etiquette by William Campbell-Everdeen
- Freemasonry in the Holy Land by Robert Morris
- A History of Masonry by George Thornburgh
- Freemasonry and its Ancient Mystic Rites by C.W. Leadbeater
- Secret Societies: A History by Arkon Daraul
- Freemasonry: A History by Angel Millar
- The Arcana of Freemasonry by Albert Churchward

- General History, Cyclopedia and Dictionary of Freemasonry by Robert Macoy
- The Secret History of the World: As Laid Down by the Secret Societies by Mark Booth
- The Rosicrucian Enlightenment by Dame Francis Yates
- Symbolism of the Compass and Square by Anonymous
- Kansas Masonic Reference Materials:
    -Blue Lodge Cipher Ritual, AF & AM
    -Royal Arch Chapter Cipher 4 Degrees Ritual and Monitor
    -Cryptic Council Cipher 2 Degrees Ritual and Monitor
    -Knight Templar Commandery Ritual Cipher 4 Degrees
    -Allied Masonic Degrees Ritual Cipher Degrees
    -Knight Masons Ritual Cipher and Monitor 3 Degrees
    -Rosicrucian Ritual of First Order
- Massachusetts Masonic Reference Materials:
    -Blue Lodge Cipher Ritual
    -Royal Arch Chapter Ritual, Monitor and Cipher
    -Royal and Select Masters Council Cipher Ritual 3 Degrees, incl. Super Excellent Master
- Miscellanea; publication of Grand Council of The Allied Masonic Degrees
- Ad Lucem; annual journal published by The Societas Rosicruciana SRICF

SUGGESTED READING
FOR
META-PROGRAMMING

- Everything is Under Control by Robert Anton Wilson (also The Cosmic Trigger 1-3)
- Science and Sanity: An Introduction to Non-Aristotelian Systems and General Semantics by Alfred Korzybski
- Cathy O' Brien and Mark Phillips:
    - *Trance*formation of America
    - Access Denied
- Behold a Pale Horse by William Cooper
- The Cloning of the American Mind: Eradicating Morality Through Education by B.K. Eakman
- The Creature from Jekyll Island by G. Edward Griffin
- Thieves in The Temple by Andre Michael Eggelletion
- The Orion Mystery by Robert Bauval
- Graham Hancock:
    - The Sign and the Seal
    - Fingerprints of the Gods
- Keeper of Genesis by Graham Hancock and Robert Bauval
- Immanuel Velikovsky:
    - Ages of Chaos
    - Worlds in Collision
- The Earth Chronicles by Zecharia Sitchin
- Vine DeLoria:
    - Evolution, Creationism, and Other Modern Myths
    - God Is Red
    - Custer Died For Your Sins
- Holger Kersten:
    - Jesus Lived in India
    - Jesus Died in Kashmir
    - The Jesus Conspiracy
- The Mythmaker: Paul and the Invention of Christianity by Hyam MacCoby
- Hamlet's Mill by Geo DeSantillana
- The Lost Language of Symbolism by Harold Bayley
- Colin Wilson:

- -Atlantis and the Kingdom of the Neanderthals: 100,000 Years of Lost History
  - -The Outsider
  - -The Atlantis Blueprint
- John Michael Greer:
  - -Mystery Teachings of the Living Earth
  - -The Druidry Handbook
  - -The Druid Magic Handbook
  - -The Celtic Golden Dawn
- Gods, Graves & Scholars: The Story of Archaeology by C.W. Ceram
- The Gods of Eden by William Bramley
- Charles Hapgood:
  - -Maps of the Ancient Sea Kings
  - -Path of the Poles
- Atlantis by Rudolph Steiner
- Gods of the Cataclysm by Hugh Fox
- The Biblical Flood and Ice Epoch by Don Pattan
- Gods, Sages, and Kings by David Frawley
- Peter Tompkins:
  - -Secrets of the Great Pyramids
  - -Mysteries of the Mexican Pyramids
  - -The Secret Life of Plants, co-written with Christopher Bird
- The Lazy Man's Guide to Enlightenment by Thaddeus Golas
- The Collected Works of Philip K. Dick, especially, The Exegesis
- The White Goddess by Robert Graves

Printed in Great Britain
by Amazon

41029516R00089